D1076306

Whitaker's Almanack
Pocket Reference

Titles published by Whitaker's Almanack

Whitaker's Almanack 2000
Whitaker's Scottish Almanack 2000
Whitaker's Almanack 1900: Facsimile Edition
*Whitaker's Almanack International Sports Records and Results
    1998/9*

Pocket-books
Whitaker's Almanack Pocket Reference
Whitaker's Almanack Pocket World 1999

Forthcoming
Whitaker's Almanack Olympic Games Encyclopaedia 2000
Whitaker's London Almanack 2000

Whitaker's
ALMANACK

POCKET
REFERENCE

LONDON: THE STATIONERY OFFICE

© The Stationery Office Ltd 1999

The Stationery Office Ltd
51 Nine Elms Lane, London SW8 5DR

First published 1998
2nd edition 1999

ISBN 0 11 702255 1

A CIP catalogue record for this book is available from the British Library

Editorial Staff
Lauren Hill (Editor)
Bridie Macmahon (Assistant Editor, UK)
Neil Mackay (Assistant Editor, UK)
Chris Sadowski (Assistant Editor, International)
Arlene Zuccolo (Database Co-ordinator)

Text designed by James Crew
Jacket designed by Compendium
Jacket photographs © Telegraph Colour Library, © Super Stock Ltd. and © PA News Ltd.
Line illustrations by Yvonne Holton
Typeset by Eclipse Design, Norwich
Printed and bound in Great Britain by William Clowes of Beccles

Foreword

If you seek the answers to questions on a wide range of subjects or have a thirst for facts, figures and general knowledge, then *Whitaker's Almanack Pocket Reference* will put this at your finger tips.

Whitaker's Almanack Pocket Reference covers everything from practical, day-to-day queries to the more esoteric enquiry. Political statistics, geographical and scientific data, historical lists, protocol, definitions ... thousands of facts and figures expertly researched and compiled.

New in this edition are diagrams of the carbon and the nitrogen cycle, listings of Secretaries-General of the United Nations and world monarchies, and terms for punctuation and accents and for animal groups.

Published in a conveniently sized, easy-to-use format, the 2nd edition of *Whitaker's Almanack Pocket Reference* is the essential tool for quizzes and general knowledge questions, whether for use in the office, or for study or leisure.

Whitaker's Almanack
51 Nine Elms Lane
London
SW8 5DR
Fax: 0171-873 8723
E-mail: whitakers.almanack@theso.co.uk

CONTENTS

MATHEMATICS

WEIGHTS AND MEASURES

MONEY

ALPHABETS AND SYMBOLS

GEOGRAPHY

THE EARTH

DIMENSIONS

Surface area = 510,069,120 km² (196,938,800 miles²), of which
  water makes up 70.92 per cent and land 29.08 per cent
Equatorial diameter = 12,756.27 km (7,926.38 miles)
Polar diameter = 12,713.50 km (7,899.80 miles)
Equatorial circumference = 40,075.01 km (24,901.46 miles)
Polar circumference = 40,007.86 km (24,859.73 miles)

Equator = 0°
North Pole = 90° N.
South Pole = 90° S.
Tropic of Cancer = 23°26′ N.
Tropic of Capricorn = 23°26′ S.
Arctic Circle = 66°34′ N.
Antarctic Circle = 66°34′ S.
The Tropics and the Arctic and Antarctic circles are affected by
the slow decrease in obliquity of the ecliptic, of about 0.5
arcseconds per year. The effect of this is that the Arctic and
Antarctic circles are currently moving towards their respective
poles by about 14 metres per year, while the Tropics move
towards the Equator by the same amount.

The Earth is divided by geologists into three layers:

Crust   thin outer layer, with an average depth of 24
         km/15 miles, although the depth varies widely
         depending on whether it is under land or sea
Mantle   lies between the crust and the core and is about
         2,865 km/1,780 miles thick
Core   extends from the mantle to the Earth's centre and
         is about 6,964 km/4,327 miles in diameter

THE ATMOSPHERE

The atmosphere is the air or mixture of gases enveloping the
Earth. Various layers are identified by scientists, based on rate of
temperature change, composition, etc. These are:
  Ionosphere (includes the thermosphere)
  Mesopause
  Mesosphere
  Stratopause
  Stratosphere (the upper atmosphere)
  Tropopause
  Troposphere (the lower atmosphere)
    (Boundary layer – up to 2 km)
  Earth's surface

Most weather conditions form in the troposphere, and this is also the layer where most pollutants released into the atmosphere by human activity accumulate. The stratosphere is the layer in which most atmospheric ozone is found.

The component gases of atmosphere are:

Gas	% by vol.
Nitrogen	78.10
Oxygen	20.95
Argon	0.934
Carbon dioxide	0.031
Neon	0.00182
Helium	0.00052
Methane	0.00020
Krypton	0.00011
Hydrogen	0.00005
Nitrous oxide	0.00005
Ozone	0.00004
Xenon	0.000009

ATMOSPHERIC POLLUTION

The Framework Convention on Climate Change was adopted by 153 states at the UN Conference on Environment and Development (UNCED) at Rio, Brazil, in 1992. It is intended to reduce the risks of global warming by limiting 'greenhouse' gas emissions. It recommended that industrialized countries reduce 'greenhouse' gas emissions to 1990 levels by 2000.

The six main 'greenhouse' gases identified by the convention are:
    carbon dioxide
    methane
    nitrous oxide
    hydrofluorocarbons (HFCs)
    perfluorocarbons (PFCs)
    sulphur hexafluoride (SF_6)

GEOLOGICAL TIME

PRECAMBRIAN ERA
*c.*4,600 – *c.*570 million years ago

Archean	Earth uninhabited
Proterozoic	First primitive life forms, e.g. algae, bacteria

PALAEOZOIC ERA ('ancient life')
*c.*570 – *c.*245 million years ago

Cambrian	Mainly sandstones, slate and shales; limestones in Scotland
	First shelled fossils and invertebrates
Ordovician	Mainly shales and mudstones, e.g. in north Wales
	First fishes
Silurian	Shales, mudstones and some limestones, found mostly in Wales and southern Scotland
Devonian	Old red sandstone, shale, limestone and slate, e.g. in south Wales and the West Country
Carboniferous	Coal-bearing rocks, millstone grit, limestone and shale
	First amphibians and insects
Permian	Marls, sandstones and clays
	Glaciations in southern continents
	First reptiles

MESOZOIC ERA ('middle forms of life')
*c.*245 – *c.*65 million years ago

Triassic	Mostly sandstone, e.g. in the West Midlands
	First mammals
Jurassic	Mainly limestones and clays, typically displayed in the Jura mountains, and in England in a NE–SW belt from Lincolnshire and the Wash to the Severn and the Dorset coast
	First birds
Cretaceous	Mainly chalk, clay and sands, e.g. in Kent and Sussex

CENOZOIC ERA ('recent life')
from *c.*65 million years ago

TERTIARY

Palaeocene	Emergence of new forms of life, including existing species
Eocene	
Oligocene	Fossils of a few still existing species
Miocene	Fossil remains show a balance of existing and extinct species

Pliocene	Fossil remains show a majority of still existing species
QUATERNARY	
Pleistocene	Glaciations and interglacials
	Majority of remains are those of still existing species
Holocene	Present, post-glacial period
	Existing species only, except for a few exterminated by man

EARTHQUAKES

Movements on or in the Earth generate seismic waves. These can be measured in a variety of ways and there are a number of different scales for comparing the relative size of earthquakes based on seismic waves, usually called seismic magnitudes. The nature of seismic waves means that any one earthquake can have many different seismic magnitudes. The main magnitude scales are:

Name	*Period of measurement (in seconds)*
Richter magnitude	0.1–1.0
body wave magnitude	1.0–5.0
surface wave magnitude	20
moment magnitude	>200

The point of initiation of an earthquake is known as the hypocentre (usually given in terms of latitude, longitude, and depth below the surface). The epicentre is the surface projection of the hypocentre.

RICHTER SCALE

Named after Charles Richter, who invented seismic magnitude scales in the 1930s.

Magnitude	*Intensity*
1	Detectable only by instruments
2	Barely detectable, even near epicentre
3	Similar to vibrations from a heavy goods vehicle
4–5	Detectable within 32 km/20 miles of the epicentre; possible slight damage within a small area
6	Moderately destructive
7	Major earthquake
8	Great earthquake

MODIFIED MERCALLI SCALE

Used mainly in Japan and most of the former Soviet republics.

Magnitude	Intensity
I	Detectable only by instruments
II	Felt by a few people at rest
III	Felt noticeably indoors; standing cars may rock
IV	Felt generally indoors; sleepers woken
V	Felt generally; plaster falls; dishes and windows broken
VI	Felt by all; chimneys and plaster damaged; objects upset
VII	Everyone runs outdoors; felt in moving cars; walls crack
VIII	General alarm; weak structures damaged; walls collapse
IX	Weak structures destroyed; ground fissured and cracked
X	Most buildings destroyed; ground badly cracked; water slopped over river banks
XI	Few buildings survive; broad fissures in ground; landslides
XII	Total destruction; waves seen on ground; objects thrown into air

WEATHER

WORLD RECORDS

AIR TEMPERATURE

Maximum	57.8°C/136°F	San Louis, Mexico, 11 August 1933
Minimum	-89.2°C/-128.56°F	Vostok, Antarctica, 21 July 1983

RAINFALL

Greatest in a day	1,870 mm/73.62 in	Cilaos, Isle de Réunion, 16 March 1952
Greatest in a calendar month	9,300 mm/366.14 in	Cherrapunji, Assam, July 1861
Greatest annual total	22,990 mm/905.12 in	Cherrapunji, Assam, 1861

WIND SPEED

Fastest gust	201 knots/231 mph	Mt Washington Observatory, USA, 12 April 1934

UK RECORDS

AIR TEMPERATURE

Maximum	37.1°C/98.8°F	Cheltenham, Glos, 3 August 1990
Minimum	-27.2°C/-17°F	Braemar, Grampian, 11 February 1895; 10 January 1982

RAINFALL

Greatest in one day	280 mm/11 in	Martinstown, Dorset, 18 July 1955
Greatest annual rainfall total	6,528 mm/257 in	Sprinkling Tarn, Cumbria, 1954

WIND SPEED

Fastest gust	150 knots/173 mph	Cairngorm, Highland, 20 March 1986
Fastest low-level gust*	123 knots/141.7 mph	Fraserburgh, Grampian, 13 February 1989

Highest mean hourly speed	92 knots/106 mph	Great Dun Fell, Cumbria, December 1974
Highest low-level mean hourly speed★	72 knots/83 mph	Shoreham-by-Sea, Sussex, 16 October 1987

★Below 200 m/656 ft

WIND FORCE MEASURES

The Beaufort Scale of wind force is used internationally in communicating weather conditions. Devised originally by Admiral Sir Francis Beaufort in 1805 as a scale of 0–12, it was extended to Force 17 by the US Weather Bureau in the 1950s. Each scale number represents a certain strength or velocity of wind at 10 m (33 ft) above ground in the open.

Scale no.	Wind force	mph	knots
0	Calm	0–1	0–1
1	Light air	1–3	1–3
2	Slight breeze	4–7	4–6
3	Gentle breeze	8–12	7–10
4	Moderate breeze	13–18	11–16
5	Fresh breeze	19–24	17–21
6	Strong breeze	25–31	22–27
7	High wind	32–38	28–33
8	Gale	39–46	34–40
9	Strong gale	47–54	41–47
10	Whole gale	55–63	48–55
11	Storm	64–72	56–63
12	Hurricane	73–82	64–71
13	—	83–92	72–80
14	—	93–103	81–89
15	—	104–114	90–99
16	—	115–125	100–108
17	—	126–136	109–118

CLOUD TYPES

Clouds comprise suspended particles of water or ice, or both. The water is condensed from air which rises into levels of lower atmospheric pressure, expands and cools to form water drops. These can remain liquid to temperatures of -30°C but below this temperature start to freeze to ice crystals. Below -40°C, clouds consist of ice crystals alone.

Clouds are classified according to the height of their base from the ground and to their shape. The basic cloud types are:

cirrus (a filament of hair)	high wispy ice clouds
stratus (a layer)	laminar, i.e. flat
cumulus (a heap or pile)	rounded, with strong vertical structure
nimbus (a rain cloud)	precipitating

The original classification scheme, devised by an English pharmacist, Luke Howard, in 1803, has been expanded to include ten cloud types:

Type (base height above ground level)	*Water phase*	*Distinctive features*
HIGH CLOUDS		
(over 5,000 m/16,500 ft)		
Cirrus (Ci)	ice	mares tails
Cirrostratus (Cs)	ice	halo cloud
Cirrocumulus (Cc)	ice or mixed	mackerel sky
MIDDLE CLOUDS		
(2,000 m/6,500 ft to 7,000 m/23,000 ft)		
Altostratus (As)	mixed or ice	overcast
Altocumulus (Ac)	liquid or mixed	widespread, cotton balls
LOW CLOUDS		
(below 2,000 m/6,500 ft)		
Nimbostratus (Ns)	mixed or ice	low, dark grey
Stratus (St)	liquid	hazy layer, like high fog
Stratocumulus (Sc)	liquid or mixed	widespread, heavy rolls
VERTICAL CLOUDS		
(1,000 m/3,000 ft to 5,000 m/16,500 ft)		
Cumulus (Cu)	liquid	fluffy, billowy
Cumulonimbus (Cb)	mixed	flat bottom, anvil- shaped top

WORLD GEOGRAPHICAL STATISTICS

OCEANS

	Area	
	km²	*miles²*
Pacific	166,240,000	64,186,300
Atlantic	86,550,000	33,420,000
Indian	73,427,000	28,350,500
Arctic	9,485,000	3,662,000

The division by the Equator of the Pacific into the North and South Pacific and the Atlantic into the North and South Atlantic makes a total of six oceans.

SEAS

	Area	
	km²	*miles²*
South China	2,974,600	1,148,500
Caribbean	2,515,900	971,400
Mediterranean	2,509,900	969,100
Bering	2,261,000	873,000
Gulf of Mexico	1,507,600	582,100
Okhotsk	1,392,000	537,500
Japan	1,012,900	391,100
Hudson Bay	730,100	281,900
East China	664,600	256,600
Andaman	564,880	218,100
Black Sea	507,900	196,100
Red Sea	453,000	174,900
North Sea	427,100	164,900
Baltic Sea	382,000	147,500
Yellow Sea	294,000	113,500
Persian Gulf	230,000	88,800

THE CONTINENTS

There are six geographic continents, although America is often divided politically into North, Central and South America.

	Area	
	km²	*miles²*
Asia	43,998,000	16,988,000
America*	41,918,000	16,185,000
Africa	29,800,000	11,506,000
Antarctica	13,209,000	5,100,000

	Area	
	km²	*miles²*
Europe†	9,699,000	3,745,000
Australia	7,618,493	2,941,526

*North and Central America have a combined area of
24,255,000 km² (9,365,000 miles²)
†Includes 5,571,000 km² (2,151,000 miles²) of former USSR
territory, including the Baltic states, Belarus, Moldova, the
Ukraine, that part of Russia west of the Ural Mountains and
Kazakhstan west of the Ural river. European Turkey (24,378
km²/9,412 miles²) comprises territory to the west and north of
the Bosporus and the Dardanelles

LARGEST ISLANDS

	Area	
	km²	*miles²*
Greenland	2,175,500	840,000
New Guinea	821,030	317,000
Borneo	725,450	280,100
Madagascar	587,040	226,658
Baffin Island	507,451	195,928
Sumatra	427,350	165,000
Honshu	227,413	87,805
Great Britain★	218,077	84,200
Victoria Island	217,292	83,897
Ellesmere Island	196,236	75,767

★Mainland only

LARGEST DESERTS

	Area (approx.)	
	km²	*miles²*
Sahara	8,400,000	3,250,000
Australian	1,550,000	600,000
Arabian	1,200,000	470,000
Gobi	1,040,000	400,000
Kalahari	520,000	200,000
Takla Makan	320,000	125,000

HIGHEST MOUNTAINS

The world's 8,000-metre mountains (with six subsidiary peaks) are all in Asia's Himalaya-Karakoram-Hindu Kush ranges.

	Height	
	metres	*feet*
Mt Everest	8,848	29,028
K2 (Chogori)†	8,607	28,238
Kangchenjunga	8,597	28,208
Lhotse	8,511	27,923
Makalu I	8,481	27,824
Lhotse Shar (II)	8,383	27,504

†Formerly Godwin-Austin

The culminating summits in the other major mountain ranges are:

Mountain (by range or country)	Height	
	metres	*feet*
Pik Pobedy, Tien Shan	7,439	24,406
Cerro Aconcagua, Andes	6,960	22,834
Mt McKinley (S. Peak), Alaska	6,194	20,320
Kilimanjaro, Tanzania	5,894	19,340
Hkakabo Razi, Myanmar	5,881	19,296
El'brus (W. Peak), Caucasus	5,642	18,510
Citlaltépetl, Mexico	5,610	18,405
Vinson Massif, Antarctica	4,897	16,066
Puncak Jaya, New Guinea	4,884	16,023
Mt Blanc, Alps	4,807	15,771

BRITISH ISLES (BY COUNTRY)

Ben Nevis, Scotland	1,344	4,406
Snowdon, Wales	1,085	3,559
Carrantuohill, Rep. of Ireland	1,050	3,414
Scafell Pike, England	977	3,210

LARGEST LAKES

The areas of some of these lakes are subject to seasonal variation.

	Area	
	km^2	$miles^2$
Caspian Sea, Iran/Azerbaijan/ Russia/Turkmenistan/Kazakhstan	371,000	143,000
Michigan-Huron, USA/Canada★	117,610	45,300
Superior, Canada/USA	82,100	31,700
Victoria, Uganda/Tanzania/Kenya	69,500	26,828
Aral Sea, Kazakhstan/Uzbekistan	40,000	15,444
Tanganyika, Dem. Rep. of Congo/ Tanzania/Zambia/Burundi	32,900	12,665
Great Bear, Canada	31,328	12,096
Baykal (Baikal), Russia†	30,500	11,776
Malawi (Nyasa), Tanzania/Malawi/ Mozambique	29,600	11,150

★Lakes Michigan and Huron are regarded as lobes of the same lake. The Michigan lobe has an area of 57,750 km^2 (22,300 $miles^2$) and the Huron lobe an area of 59,570 km^2 (23,000 $miles^2$)
†World's deepest lake (1,940 m/6,365 ft)

UNITED KINGDOM (BY COUNTRY)

Lough Neagh, Northern Ireland	381.73	147.39
Loch Lomond, Scotland	71.12	27.46
Windermere, England	14.74	5.69
Lake Vyrnwy (artificial), Wales	4.53	1.75
Llyn Tegid (Bala) (natural), Wales	4.38	1.69

LONGEST RIVERS

	Length	
	km	miles
Nile, Africa	6,670	4,145
Amazon, S. America	6,448	4,007
Yangtze-Kiang (Chang Jiang), China	6,380	3,964
Mississippi-Missouri-Red Rock, N. America	5,970	3,710
Yenisey-Angara, Mongolia/Russia	5,540	3,442
Huang He (Yellow River), China	5,463	3,395

	Length	
	km	*miles*
BRITISH ISLES (BY COUNTRY)		
Shannon, Rep. of Ireland	386	240
Severn, Britain	354	220
Thames, England	346	215
Tay, Scotland	188	117
Bann (Upper and Lower), N. Ireland	122	76

HIGHEST WATERFALLS

	Total drop	
	metres	*feet*
Saltó Angel, Venezuela	979	3,212
Tugela, S. Africa	914	2,014
Utigård, Norway	800	2,625
Mongefossen, Norway	774	2,540
Yosemite, USA	739	2,425
Østre Mardøla Foss, Norway	656	2,154
BRITISH ISLES (BY COUNTRY)		
Eas a' Chuàl Aluinn, Scotland	200	658
Powerscourt Falls, Rep. of Ireland	106	350
Pistyll-y-Llyn, Wales*	72	*c.*235
Pistyll Rhyadr, Wales	71.5	235
Caldron Snout, England*	61	200

* cascades

PLACES

COUNTRIES OF THE WORLD

Country name	Area
Afghanistan	251,773 miles^2/652,090 km^2
Albania	11,099 miles^2/28,748 km^2
Algeria	919,595 miles^2/2,381,741 km^2
American Samoa (USA)	77 miles^2/199 km^2
Andorra	175 miles^2/453 km^2
Angola	481,354 miles^2/1,246,700 km^2
Anguilla (UK)	37 miles^2/96 km^2
Antigua and Barbuda	171 miles^2/442 km^2
Argentina	1,073,518 miles^2/2,780,400 km^2
Armenia	11,506 miles^2/29,800 km^2
Aruba (Netherlands)	75 miles^2/193 km^2
Ascension Island (UK)	34 miles^2/88 km^2
Australia	2,988,902 miles^2/7,741,220 km^2
Norfolk Island	14 miles^2/36 km^2
Austria	32,378 miles^2/83,859 km^2
Azerbaijan	33,436 miles^2/86,600 km^2
The Bahamas	5,358 miles^2/13,878 km^2
Bahrain	268 miles^2/694 km^2
Bangladesh	55,598 miles^2/143,998 km^2
Barbados	166 miles^2/430 km^2
Belarus	80,155 miles^2/207,600 km^2
Belgium	11,783 miles^2/30,519 km^2
Belize	8,763 miles^2/22,696 km^2
Benin	43,484 miles^2/112,622 km^2
Bermuda (UK)	20 miles^2/53 km^2
Bhutan	18,147 miles^2/47,000 km^2
Bolivia	424,165 miles^2/1,098,581 km^2
Bosnia-Hercegovina	19,741 miles^2/51,129 km^2
Botswana	224,607 miles^2/581,730 km^2
Brazil	3,300,171 miles^2/8,547,403 km^2
Brunei	2,226 miles^2/5,765 km^2
Bulgaria	42,823 miles^2/110,912 km^2
Burkina Faso	105,792 miles^2/274,000 km^2
Burundi	10,747 miles^2/27,834 km^2
Cambodia	69,898 miles^2/181,035 km^2
Cameroon	183,569 miles^2/475,442 km^2
Canada	3,849,674 miles^2/9,970,610 km^2
Cape Verde	1,557 miles^2/4,033 km^2
Cayman Islands (UK)	102 miles^2/264 km^2
Central African Republic	240,535 miles^2/622,984 km^2
Chad	495,755 miles^2/1,284,000 km^2

Population	Capital (*Seaport)
20,883,000	Kabul
3,670,000	Tirana
29,168,000	*Algiers
56,000	*Pago Pago
65,877	Andorra la Vella
11,185,000	*Luanda
12,394	The Valley
66,000	*St John's
35,220,000	*Buenos Aires
3,893,000	Yerevan
71,000	*Oranjestad
1,051	*Georgetown
18,871,800	Canberra
1,772	*Kingston
8,106,000	Vienna
7,625,000	*Baku
284,000	*Nassau
599,000	*Manama
120,073,000	Dhaka
265,000	*Bridgetown
10,203,000	Minsk
10,159,000	Brussels
222,000	Belmopan
5,563,000	*Porto Novo
64,000	*Hamilton
1,812,000	Thimphu
8,140,000	La Paz
4,510,000	Sarajevo
1,490,000	Gaborone
157,872,000	Brasilia
300,000	Bandar Seri Begawan
8,356,000	Sofia
10,780,000	Ouagadougou
6,088,000	Bujumbura
10,273,000	*Phnom Penh
13,560,000	Yaoundé
29,964,000	Ottawa
396,000	*Praia
38,000	*George Town
3,344,000	Bangui
6,515,000	N'Djaména

Country name	*Area*
Chile	292,135 miles²/756,626 km²
China	3,705,408 miles²/9,596,961 km²
Hong Kong	415 miles²/1,075 km²
Colombia	439,737 miles²/1,138,914 km²
The Comoros	863 miles²/2,235 km²
Congo, Democratic Republic
of (formerly Zaïre)	905,355 miles²/2,344,858 km²
Congo, Republic of	132,047 miles²/342,000 km²
Costa Rica	19,730 miles²/51,100 km²
Côte d'Ivoire	124,504 miles²/322,463 km²
Croatia	34,022 miles²/88,117 km²
Cuba	42,804 miles²/110,861 km²
Cyprus	3,572 miles²/9,251 km²
Czech Republic	30,450 miles²/78,864 km²
Denmark	16,639 miles²/43,094 km²
Faröe Islands	540 miles²/1,399 km²
Djibouti	8,958 miles²/23,200 km²
Dominica	290 miles²/751 km²
Dominican Republic	18,816 miles²/48,734 km²
Ecuador	109,484 miles²/283,561 km²
Egypt	386,662 miles²/1,001,449 km²
El Salvador	8,124 miles²/21,041 km²
Equatorial Guinea	10,831 miles²/28,051 km²
Eritrea	45,406 miles²/117,600 km²
Estonia	17,413 miles²/45,100 km²
Ethiopia	426,373 miles²/1,104,300 km²
Falkland Islands (UK)	4,700 miles²/12,173 km²
Fiji	7,056 miles²/18,274 km²
Finland	130,559 miles²/338,145 km²
France	212,935 miles²/551,500 km²
French Guiana (France)	34,749 miles²/90,000 km²
French Polynesia (France)	1,544 miles²/4,000 km²
Gabon	103,347 miles²/267,668 km²
The Gambia	4,361 miles²/11,295 km²
Georgia	26,911 miles²/69,700 km²
Germany	137,735 miles²/356,733 km²
Ghana	92,098 miles²/238,533 km²
Gibraltar (UK)	23 miles²/6 km²
Greece	50,949 miles²/131,957 km²
Greenland (Denmark)	840,004 miles²/2,175,600 km²
Grenada	133 miles²/344 km²
Guadeloupe (France)	658 miles²/1,705 km²
Guam (USA)	212 miles²/549 km²
Guatemala	42,042 miles²/108,889 km²

Population	Capital (*Seaport)
14,419,000	Santiago
1,232,083,000	Beijing/Peking
6,311,000	—
35,626,000	Bogotá
632,000	Moroni
46,812,000	Kinshasa
2,668,000	Brazzaville
3,398,000	San José
14,781,000	Yamoussoukro
4,501,000	Zagreb
11,019,000	*Havana
756,000	Nicosia
10,315,000	Prague
5,262,000	*Copenhagen
47,000	*Tórshavn
617,000	*Djibouti
74,000	*Roseau
8,052,000	*Santo Domingo
11,698,000	Quito
60,603,000	Cairo
5,796,000	San Salvador
400,000	*Malabo
3,280,000	Asmara
1,470,000	Tallinn
58,506,000	Addis Ababa
2,221	*Stanley
797,000	*Suva
5,125,000	*Helsinki
58,375,000	Paris
153,000	*Cayenne
223,000	*Papeete
1,106,000	*Libreville
1,141,000	*Banjul
5,411,000	Tbilisi
81,912,000	Berlin
17,832,000	*Accra
27,192	*Gibraltar
10,475,000	Athens
58,000	*Godthåb
92,000	*St George's
431,000	*Basse Terre
153,000	Agaña
10,928,000	Guatemala City

Country name	Area
Guinea	94,926 miles^2/245,857 km^2
Guinea-Bissau	13,948 miles^2/36,125 km^2
Guyana	83,000 miles^2/214,969 km^2
Haiti	10,714 miles^2/27,750 km^2
Honduras	43,277 miles^2/112,088 km^2
Hungary	35,920 miles^2/93,032 km^2
Iceland	39,769 miles^2/103,000 km^2
India	1,269,346 miles^2/3,287,590 km^2
Indonesia	735,358 miles^2/1,904,569 km^2
Iran	630,577 miles^2/1,633,188 km^2
Iraq	169,235 miles^2/438,317 km^2
Ireland, Republic of	27,137 miles^2/70,284 km^2
Israel	8,130 miles^2/21,056 km^2
West Bank and Gaza Strip	2,406 miles^2/6,231 km^2
Italy	116,320 miles^2/301,268 km^2
Jamaica	4,243 miles^2/10,990 km^2
Japan	145,870 miles^2/377,801 km^2
Jordan	37,738 miles^2/97,740 km^2
Kazakhstan	1,049,156 miles^2/2,717,300 km^2
Kenya	224,081 miles^2/580,367 km^2
Kiribati	280 miles^2/726 km^2
Korea, Democratic People's Republic of (North)	46,540 miles^2/120,538 km^2
Korea, Republic of (South)	38,330 miles^2/99,274 km^2
Kuwait	6,880 miles^2/17,818 km^2
Kyrgyzstan	76,641 miles^2/198,500 km^2
Laos	91,429 miles^2/236,800 km^2
Latvia	24,942 miles^2/64,600 km^2
Lebanon	4,015 miles^2/10,400 km^2
Lesotho	11,720 miles^2/30,355 km^2
Liberia	43,000 miles^2/111,369 km^2
Libya	679,362 miles^2/1,759,540 km^2
Liechtenstein	62 miles^2/160 km^2
Lithuania	25,174 miles^2/65,200 km^2
Luxembourg	998 miles^2/2,586 km^2
Macao (Portugal)	7 miles^2/18 km^2
Macedonia, Former Yugoslav Republic of	9,928 miles^2/25,713 km^2
Madagascar	226,658 miles^2/587,041 km^2
Malawi	45,747 miles^2/118,484 km^2
Malaysia	127,320 miles^2/329,758 km^2
Maldives	115 miles^2/298 km^2
Mali	478,841 miles^2/1,240,192 km^2
Malta	122 miles^2/316 km^2

Population	Capital (*Seaport)
7,518,000	*Conakry
1,091,000	*Bissau
838,000	*Georgetown
7,336,000	*Port-au-Prince
6,140,000	Tegucigalpa
10,193,000	Budapest
272,064	*Reykjavik
936,000,000	New Delhi
196,813,000	*Jakarta
61,128,000	Tehran
20,607,000	Baghdad
3,626,000	*Dublin
5,696,000	Tel Aviv
1,635,000	Gaza City
57,339,000	Rome
2,491,000	*Kingston
125,761,000	Tokyo
5,581,000	Amman
16,526,000	Astana
31,806,000	Nairobi
80,000	Tarawa
22,466,000	Pyongyang
45,545,000	Seoul
1,687,000	*Kuwait City
4,575,000	Bishkek
5,035,000	Vientiane
2,491,000	Riga
3,084,000	*Beirut
2,078,000	Maseru
2,820,000	*Monrovia
5,593,000	*Tripoli
31,000	Vaduz
3,710,000	Vilnius
412,000	Luxembourg
440,000	*Macao
2,174,000	Skopje
15,353,000	Antananarivo
10,114,000	Lilongwe
20,581,000	Kuala Lumpur
263,000	*Malé
11,134,000	Bamako
373,000	*Valletta

Country name   *Area*

Marshall Islands	70 miles²/181 km²
Martinique (France)	425 miles²/1,102 km²
Mauritania	395,956 miles²/1,025,520 km²
Mauritius	788 miles²/2,040 km²
Mayotte (France)	144 miles²/372 km²
Mexico	756,066 miles²/1,958,201 km²
Micronesia, Federated States of	271 miles²/702 km²
Moldova	13,012 miles²/33,700 km²
Monaco	0.4 miles²/1 km²
Mongolia	604,829 miles²/1,566,500 km²
Montserrat (UK)	39 miles²/102 km²
Morocco	172,414 miles²/446,550 km²
Western Sahara	102,703 miles²/266,000 km²
Mozambique	309,496 miles²/801,590 km²
Myanmar (formerly Burma)	261,228 miles²/676,578 km²
Namibia	318,261 miles²/824,292 km²
Nauru	8 miles²/21 km²
Nepal	56,827 miles²/147,181 km²
The Netherlands	15,770 miles²/40,844 km²
Netherlands Antilles	309 miles²/800 km²
New Caledonia	7,172 miles²/18,575 km²
New Zealand	104,454 miles²/270,534 km²
Cook Islands	91 miles²/236 km²
Niue	100 miles²/260 km²
Ross Dependency	175,000 miles²/453,248 km²
Tokelau	5 miles²/12 km²
Nicaragua	50,193 miles²/130,000 km²
Niger	489,191 miles²/1,267,000 km²
Nigeria	356,669 miles²/923,768 km²
Northern Mariana Islands (USA)	179 miles²/464 km²
Norway	125,050 miles²/323,877 km²
Oman	82,030 miles²/212,457 km²
Pakistan	307,374 miles²/796,095 km²
Palau (USA)	177 miles²/459 km²
Panama	29,157 miles²/75,517 km²
Papua New Guinea	178,704 miles²/462,840 km²
Paraguay	157,048 miles²/406,752 km²
Peru	496,225 miles²/1,285,216 km²
The Philippines	115,831 miles²/300,000 km²
Pitcairn Islands (UK)	2 miles²/5 km²
Poland	124,808 miles²/323,250 km²
Portugal	35,514 miles²/91,982 km²
Puerto Rico (USA)	3,427 miles²/8,875 km²

Population	Capital (*Seaport)
58,000	Dalap-Uliga-Darrit
384,000	*Fort de France
2,351,000	Nouakchott
1,134,000	*Port Louis
94,410	Mamoundzou
96,578,000	Mexico City
109,000	Palikir
4,327,000	Kishinev
32,000	Monaco
2,354,000	Ulan Bator
4,500	*Plymouth
27,623,000	*Rabat
256,000	Laayoune
17,796,000	*Maputo
45,922,000	*Yangon/Rangoon
1,575,000	Windhoek
11,000	*Nauru
21,127,000	Kathmandu
15,517,000	*Amsterdam
195,000	*Willemstad
189,000	*Noumea
3,681,546	*Wellington
19,000	Rarotonga
2,000	Alofi
—	—
2,000	—
4,238,000	Managua
9,465,000	Niamey
115,120,000	Abuja
49,000	Saipan
4,381,000	*Oslo
2,302,000	*Muscat
134,146,000	Islamabad
17,000	Koror
2,674,000	*Panama City
4,400,000	*Port Moresby
4,955,000	Asunción
23,947,000	Lima
71,899,000	*Manila
54	—
38,628,000	Warsaw
9,920,760	*Lisbon
3,736,000	*San Juan

Country name   *Area*

Qatar   4,247 miles^2/11,000 km^2
Réunion (France)   969 miles^2/2,510 km^2
Romania   92,043 miles^2/238,391 km^2
Russia   6,592,850 miles^2/17,075,400 km^2
Rwanda   10,169 miles^2/26,338 km^2
St Christopher and Nevis   101 miles^2/261 km^2
St Helena (UK)   47 miles^2/122 km^2
St Lucia   240 miles^2/622 km^2
St Pierre and Miquelon (France)   93 miles^2/242 km^2
St Vincent and The Grenadines   150 miles^2/388 km^2
Samoa   1,093 miles^2/2,831 km^2
San Marino   24 miles^2/61 km^2
São Tomé and Princípe   372 miles^2/964 km^2
Saudi Arabia   830,000 miles^2/2,149,690 km^2
Senegal   75,955 miles^2/196,722 km^2
Seychelles   176 miles^2/455 km^2
Sierra Leone   27,699 miles^2/71,740 km^2
Singapore   239 miles^2/618 km^2
Slovakia   18,924 miles^2/49,012 km^2
Slovenia   7,821 miles^2/20,256 km^2
Solomon Islands   11,157 miles^2/28,896 km^2
Somalia   246,201 miles^2/637,657 km^2
South Africa   471,445 miles^2/1,221,037 km^2
South Georgia (UK)   1,580 miles^2/4,092 km^2
Spain   195,365 miles^2/505,992 km^2
Sri Lanka   25,332 miles^2/65,610 km^2
Sudan   967,500 miles^2/2,505,813 km^2
Suriname   63,037 miles^2/163,265 km^2
Swaziland   6,704 miles^2/17,364 km^2
Sweden   173,732 miles^2/449,964 km^2
Switzerland   15,940 miles^2/41,284 km^2
Syria   71,498 miles^2/185,180 km^2
Taiwan   13,800 miles^2/35,742 km^2
Tajikistan   55,251 miles^2/143,100 km^2
Tanzania   341,217 miles^2/883,749 km^2
Thailand   198,115 miles^2/513,115 km^2
Togo   21,925 miles^2/56,785 km^2
Tonga   288 miles^2/747 km^2
Trinidad and Tobago   1,981 miles^2/5,130 km^2
Tristan da Cunha (UK)   38 miles^2/98 km^2
Tunisia   63,170 miles^2/163,610 km^2
Turkey   299,158 miles2/774,815 km2
Turkmenistan   188,456 miles^2/488,100 km^2
Turks and Caicos Islands (UK)   166 miles^2/430 km^2

Population	*Capital (★Seaport)*
558,000	★Doha
664,000	St Denis
22,608,000	Bucharest
147,739,000	Moscow
5,397,000	Kigali
41,000	★Basseterre
5,157	★Jamestown
144,000	★Castries
7,000	★St Pierre
113,000	★Kingstown
166,000	★Apia
25,000	San Marino
135,000	★São Tomé
18,836,000	Riyadh
8,572,000	★Dakar
76,000	★Victoria
4,297,000	★Freetown
3,044,000	—
5,374,000	Bratislava
1,991,000	Ljubljana
391,000	★Honiara
9,822,000	★Mogadishu
42,393,000	Pretoria/★Cape Town
—	—
39,270,000	Madrid
18,354,000	Colombo
27,291,000	Khartoum
423,000	★Paramaribo
938,000	Mbabane
8,843,000	★Stockholm
7,076,000	Berne
14,619,000	Damascus
21,450,183	Taipei
5,919,000	Dushanbe
30,799,000	Dodoma
60,206,000	★Bangkok
4,201,000	★Lomé
99,000	★Nuku'alofa
1,297,000	★Port of Spain
288	★Edinburgh of the Seven Seas
9,092,000	★Tunis
62,697,000	Ankara
4,569,000	Ashkhabad
23,000	★Grand Turk

Country name	*Area*
Tuvalu	10 miles^2/26 km^2
Uganda	93,065 miles^2/241,038 km^2
Ukraine	233,090 miles^2/603,700 km^2
United Arab Emirates	32,278 miles^2/83,600 km^2
United Kingdom	94,248 miles^2/244,101 km^2
England	50,351 miles^2/130,410 km^2
Wales	8,015 miles^2/20,758 km^2
Scotland	30,420 miles^2/78,789 km^2
Northern Ireland	5,467 miles^2/14,160 km^2
United States of America	3,615,276 miles^2/9,363,520 km^2
Uruguay	68,500 miles^2/177,414 km^2
Uzbekistan	172,742 miles^2/447,400 km^2
Vanuatu	4,706 miles^2/12,189 km^2
Vatican City State	0.2 miles^2/0.44 km^2
Venezuela	352,145 miles^2/912,050 km^2
Vietnam	128,066 miles^2/331,689 km^2
Virgin Islands, British (UK)	58 miles^2/151 km^2
Virgin Islands, US (USA)	134 miles^2/347 km^2
Wallis and Futuna Islands (France)	77 miles^2/200 km^2
Yemen	203,850 miles^2/527,968 km^2
Yugoslavia, Federal Republic of	39,449 miles^2/102,173 km^2
Zambia	290,587 miles^2/752,618 km^2
Zimbabwe	150,872 miles^2/390,757 km^2

Population	*Capital (*Seaport)*
10,000	*Funafuti
19,848,000	Kampala
51,094,000	Kiev
2,260,000	Abu Dhabi
58,784,000	*London
48,903,000	*London
2,917,000	*Cardiff
5,137,000	*Edinburgh
1,649,000	*Belfast
266,557,000	Washington DC
3,203,000	*Montevideo
22,912,000	Tashkent
169,000	*Port Vila
1,000	Vatican City
22,710,000	Caracas
75,181,000	Hanoi
19,000	*Road Town
106,000	*Charlotte Amalie
15,000	*Mata-Utu
15,919,00	Sana'a
10,574,000	Belgrade
8,275,000	Lusaka
11,908,000	Harare

STATES OF THE USA

	Abbreviation	Zip code	Capital
Alabama	Ala.	AL	Montgomery
Alaska		AK	Juneau
Arizona	Ariz.	AZ	Phoenix
Arkansas	Ark.	AR	Little Rock
California	Calif.	CA	Sacramento
Colorado	Colo.	CO	Denver
★Connecticut	Conn.	CT	Hartford
★Delaware	Del.	DE	Dover
Florida	Fla.	FL	Tallahassee
★Georgia	Ga.	GA	Atlanta
Hawaii		HI	Honolulu
Idaho		ID	Boise
Illinois	Ill.	IL	Springfield
Indiana	Ind.	IN	Indianapolis
Iowa		IA	Des Moines
Kansas	Kan.	KS	Topeka
Kentucky	Ky.	KY	Frankfort
Louisiana	La.	LA	Baton Rouge
Maine	Me.	ME	Augusta
★Maryland	Md.	MD	Annapolis
★Massachusetts	Mass.	MA	Boston
Michigan	Mich.	MI	Lansing
Minnesota	Minn.	MN	St Paul
Mississippi	Miss.	MS	Jackson
Missouri	Mo.	MO	Jefferson City
Montana	Mont.	MT	Helena
Nebraska	Neb.	NE	Lincoln
Nevada	Nev.	NV	Carson City
★New Hampshire	NH	NH	Concord
★New Jersey	NJ	NJ	Trenton
New Mexico	N.Mex./NM	NM	Santa Fé
★New York	NY	NY	Albany
★North Carolina	NC	NC	Raleigh
North Dakota	N.Dak./ ND	ND	Bismarck
Ohio		OH	Columbus
Oklahoma	Okla.	OK	Oklahoma City
Oregon	Ore.	OR	Salem
★Pennsylvania	Pa./Penn./ Penna.	PA	Harrisburg
★Rhode Island	RI	RI	Providence
★South Carolina	SC	SC	Columbia
South Dakota	S.Dak./SD	SD	Pierre
Tennessee	Tenn.	TN	Nashville
Texas	Tex.	TX	Austin

	Abbreviation	*Zip code*	*Capital*
Utah		UT	Salt Lake City
Vermont	Vt.	VT	Montpelier
★Virginia	Va.	VA	Richmond
Washington	Wash.	WA	Olympia
West Virginia	W.Va.	WV	Charleston
Wisconsin	Wis.	WI	Madison
Wyoming	Wyo	WY	Cheyenne
District of Columbia	DC	DC	

★The 13 original states

STATES AND TERRITORIES OF AUSTRALIA

	Abbreviation	*Capital*
Australian Capital Territory	ACT	Canberra
New South Wales	NSW	Sydney
Northern Territory	NT	Darwin★
Queensland	Qld	Brisbane
South Australia	SA	Adelaide
Tasmania	Tas.	Hobart
Victoria	Vic.	Melbourne
Western Australia	WA	Perth

★Seat of administration

PROVINCES AND TERRITORIES OF CANADA

	Abbreviation	*Capital*
Alberta	AB	Edmonton
British Columbia	BC	Victoria
Manitoba	MB	Winnipeg
New Brunswick	NB	Fredericton
Newfoundland and Labrador	NF	St John's
Northwest Territories	NT	Yellowknife★
Nova Scotia	NS	Halifax
Nunavut	NT	Iqaluit
Ontario	ON	Toronto
Prince Edward Island	PE	Charlottetown
Quebec	QC	Quebec
Saskatchewan	SK	Regina
Yukon Territory	YT	Whitehorse★

★Seat of government

DISTANCES FROM LONDON BY AIR

The list of the distances in statute miles from London, Heathrow,
to various cities (airport) abroad has been supplied by the
publishers of IATA/Serco Aviation Services Air Distances Manual,
Southall, Middx.

To	Miles
Abidjan	3,197
Abu Dhabi (International)	3,425
Addis Ababa	3,675
Adelaide (International)	10,111
Aden	3,670
Algiers	1,035
Amman (Queen Alia)	2,287
Amsterdam	230
Ankara (Esenboga)	1,770
Athens	1,500
Atlanta	4,198
Auckland	11,404
Baghdad (Saddam)	2,551
Bahrain	3,163
Baku	2,485
Bangkok	5,928
Barbados	4,193
Barcelona (Muntadas)	712
Basle	447
Beijing (Capital)	5,063
Beirut	2,161
Belfast (Aldergrove)	325
Belgrade	1,056
Berlin (Tegel)	588
Bermuda	3,428
Berne	476
Bogotá	5,262
Bombay (Mumbai)	4,478
Boston	3,255
Brasilia	5,452
Bratislava	817
Brisbane (Eagle Farm)	10,273
Brussels	217
Bucharest (Otopeni)	1,307
Budapest	923
Buenos Aires	6,915
Cairo (International)	2,194
Calcutta	4,958
Calgary	4,357

To	Miles
Canberra	10,563
Cape Town	6,011
Caracas	4,639
Casablanca (Mohamed V)	1,300
Chicago (O'Hare)	3,941
Cologne	331
Colombo (Katunayake)	5,411
Copenhagen	608
Dakar	2,706
Dallas (Fort Worth)	4,736
Dallas (Lovefield)	4,732
Damascus (International)	2,223
Dar-es-Salaam	4,662
Darwin	8,613
Delhi	4,180
Denver	4,655
Detroit (Metropolitan)	3,754
Dhahran	3,143
Dhaka	4,976
Doha	3,253
Dubai	3,414
Dublin	279
Durban	5,937
Düsseldorf	310
Entebbe	4,033
Frankfurt (Main)	406
Freetown	3,046
Geneva	468
Gibraltar	1,084
Gothenburg (Landvetter)	664
Hamburg	463
Harare	5,156
Havana	4,647
Helsinki (Vantaa)	1,148
Hobart	10,826
Ho Chi Minh City	6,345
Hong Kong	5,990
Honolulu	7,220
Houston (Intercontinental)	4,821
Houston (William P. Hobby)	4,837
Islamabad	3,767
Istanbul	1,560
Jakarta (Halim Perdanakusuma)	7,295
Jeddah	2,947
Johannesburg	5,634
Kabul	3,558

To	Miles
Karachi	3,935
Kathmandu	4,570
Khartoum	3,071
Kiev (Borispol)	1,357
Kiev (Julyany)	1,337
Kingston, Jamaica	4,668
Kuala Lumpur (Subang)	6,557
Kuwait	2,903
Lagos	3,107
Larnaca	2,036
Lima	6,303
Lisbon	972
Lomé	3,129
Los Angeles (International)	5,439
Madras	5,113
Madrid	773
Malta	1,305
Manila	6,685
Marseille	614
Mauritius	6,075
Melbourne (Essendon)	10,504
Melbourne (Tullamarine)	10,499
Mexico City	5,529
Miami	4,414
Milan (Linate)	609
Minsk	1,176
Montego Bay	4,687
Montevideo	6,841
Montreal (Mirabel)	3,241
Moscow (Sheremetievo)	1,557
Munich (Franz Josef Strauss)	584
Muscat	3,621
Nairobi (Jomo Kenyatta)	4,248
Naples	1,011
Nassau	4,333
New York (J. F. Kennedy)	3,440
Nice	645
Oporto	806
Oslo (Fornebu)	722
Ottawa	3,321
Palma, Majorca (Son San Juan)	836
Paris (Charles de Gaulle)	215
Paris (Le Bourget)	215
Paris (Orly)	227
Perth, Australia	9,008
Port of Spain	4,404

To	Miles
Prague	649
Pretoria	5,602
Reykjavik (Domestic)	1,167
Reykjavik (Keflavik)	1,177
Rhodes	1,743
Rio de Janeiro	5,745
Riyadh (King Khaled) International	3,067
Rome (Fiumicino)	895
St John's, Newfoundland	2,308
St Petersburg	1,314
Salzburg	651
San Francisco	5,351
Saõ Paulo	5,892
Sarajevo	1,017
Seoul (Kimpo)	5,507
Shanghai	5,725
Shannon	369
Singapore (Changi)	6,756
Sofia	1,266
Stockholm (Arlanda)	908
Suva	10,119
Sydney (Kingsford Smith)	10,568
Tangier	1,120
Tehran	2,741
Tel Aviv	2,227
Tokyo (Narita)	5,956
Toronto	3,544
Tripoli (International)	1,468
Tunis	1,137
Turin (Caselle)	570
Ulan Bator	4,340
Valencia	826
Vancouver	4,707
Venice (Tessera)	715
Vienna (Schwechat)	790
Vladivostok	5,298
Warsaw	912
Washington (Dulles)	3,665
Wellington	11,692
Yangon/Rangoon	5,582
Yokohama (Aomori)	5,647
Zagreb	848
Zürich	490

THE UNITED KINGDOM

AREA

The United Kingdom comprises Great Britain (England, Wales and Scotland) and Northern Ireland.

The Isle of Man and the Channel Islands are Crown dependencies with their own legislative systems, and not part of the United Kingdom.

AREA AS AT 31 MARCH 1981

	miles²	km²
United Kingdom	94,248	244,101
England	50,351	130,410
Wales	8,015	20,758
Scotland	30,420	78,789
Northern Ireland*	5,467	14,160
Isle of Man	221	572
Channel Islands	75	194

*Excluding certain tidal waters that are parts of statutory areas in Northern Ireland

POPULATION

The first official census of population in England, Wales and Scotland was taken in 1801 and a census has been taken every ten years since, except in 1941 when there was no census because of war. The last official census in the United Kingdom was taken on 21 April 1991 and the next is due in April 2001.

The first official census of population in Ireland was taken in 1841. However, all figures given below refer only to the area which is now Northern Ireland. Figures for Northern Ireland in 1921 and 1931 are estimates based on the censuses taken in 1926 and 1937 respectively.

Estimates of the population of England before 1801, calculated from the number of baptisms, burials and marriages, are:

1570	4,160,221
1600	4,811,718
1630	5,600,517
1670	5,773,646
1700	6,045,008
1750	6,517,035

UK CENSUS RESULTS 1801–1991

	Total	Male	Female
1801	—	—	—
1811	13,368,000	6,368,000	7,000,000
1821	15,472,000	7,498,000	7,974,000

	Total	Male	Female
1831	17,835,000	8,647,000	9,188,000
1841	20,183,000	9,819,000	10,364,000
1851	22,259,000	10,855,000	11,404,000
1861	24,525,000	11,894,000	12,631,000
1871	27,431,000	13,309,000	14,122,000
1881	31,015,000	15,060,000	15,955,000
1891	34,264,000	16,593,000	17,671,000
1901	38,237,000	18,492,000	19,745,000
1911	42,082,000	20,357,000	21,725,000
1921	44,027,000	21,033,000	22,994,000
1931	46,038,000	22,060,000	23,978,000
1951	50,225,000	24,118,000	26,107,000
1961	52,709,000	25,481,000	27,228,000
1971	55,515,000	26,952,000	28,562,000
1981	55,848,000	27,104,000	28,742,000
1991	56,467,000	27,344,000	29,123,000

PROJECTED POPULATION*

	Total	Male	Female
2001	59,618,000	29,377,000	30,160,000
2011	60,929,000	30,206,000	30,483,000
2021	62,244,000	30,916,000	30,754,000

*Projections are 1996 based

RESIDENT POPULATION: MID-YEAR ESTIMATE

	1987	1997
United Kingdom	57,009,000	59,009,000
England	47,448,000	49,284,000
Wales	2,833,000	2,927,000
Scotland	5,113,000	5,123,000
Northern Ireland	1,575,000	1,675,000

AVERAGE DENSITY: PERSONS PER HECTARE

	1981	1991
England	3.55	3.61
Wales	1.34	1.36
Scotland	0.66	0.65
Northern Ireland	1.12	1.11

CAUSES OF DEATH 1997

	All ages
Males	
Circulatory diseases	41%
Cancer	27%
Respiratory diseases	15%
Injury and poisoning	4%

	All ages
Infectious diseases	1%
Other causes	11%
All males (100%)	300,400

Females	
Circulatory diseases	41%
Cancer	23%
Respiratory diseases	17%
Injury and poisoning	2%
Infectious diseases	1%
Other causes	16%
All females (100%)	329,300

THE ANCIENT WORLD

THE SEVEN WONDERS OF THE WORLD

The following sights were identified by classical observers as the pre-eminent architectural and sculptural achievements of the ancient world. Only the pyramids of Egypt are still in existence.

I THE PYRAMIDS OF EGYPT

The pyramids are found from Gizeh, near Cairo, to a southern limit 60 miles (96 km) distant. The oldest is that of Zoser, at Saqqara, built c.2650 BC. The Great Pyramid of Cheops (built c.2580 BC) covers 13.12 acres (756 x 756 ft or 230.4 x 230.4 m) at the base and was originally 481 ft (146.6 m) in height.

II THE HANGING GARDENS OF BABYLON

These adjoined Nebuchadnezzar's palace, 60 miles (96 km) south of Baghdad. The terraced gardens, ranging from 75 ft to 300 ft (25–90 m) above ground level, were watered from storage tanks on the highest terrace.

III THE TOMB OF MAUSOLUS

Built at Halicarnassus, in Asia Minor, by the widowed Queen Artemisia about 350 BC. The memorial originated the term mausoleum.

IV THE TEMPLE OF ARTEMIS AT EPHESUS

Ionic temple erected about 350 BC in honour of the goddess and burned by the Goths in AD 262.

V THE COLOSSUS OF RHODES

A bronze statue of Apollo, set up about 280 BC. According to legend it stood at the harbour entrance of the seaport of Rhodes.

VI THE STATUE OF ZEUS

Located at Olympia in the plain of Elis, and constructed of marble inlaid with ivory and gold by the sculptor Phidias, about 430 BC.

VII THE PHAROS OF ALEXANDRIA

A marble watch tower and lighthouse on the island of Pharos in the harbour of Alexandria, built c.270 BC.

ROMAN NAMES

The following is a list of the Roman names for geographical areas and features and for towns and settlements. The area to which the Roman name for a town or country referred is not necessarily precisely the same area occupied by the modern town or country.

THE BRITISH ISLES

Abergavenny	*Gobannium*
Aldborough	*Isurium Brigantum*
Ambleside	*Galava*
Ancaster	*Causennae*
Anglesey	*Mona*
Armagh	*Armacha*
Avon, R.	*Auvona*
Bath	*Aquae Sulis*
Brancaster	*Branodunum*
Britain	*Britannia*
Caerleon	*Isca*
Caerwent	*Venta Silurum*
Canterbury	*Durovernum Cantiacorum*
Cardigan	*Ceretica*
Carlisle	*Luguvalium*
Carmarthen	*Maridunum*
Carnarvon	*Segontium*
Chelmsford	*Caesaromagus*
Chester	*Deva*
Chichester	*Noviomagus Regnensium*
Cirencester	*Corinium Dobunnorum*
Clyde, R.	*Clota*
Colchester	*Camulodunum*
Corbridge	*Corstopitum*
Dee, R.	*Deva*
Doncaster	*Danum*
Dorchester	*Durnovaria*
Dover	*Dubris*
Dover, Straits of	*Fretum Gallicum*
Dunstable	*Durocobrivae*
Eden, R.	*Ituna*
England	*Anglia*
Exeter	*Isca Dumnoniorum*
Forth, R.	*Bodotria*
Gloucester	*Glevum*
Hebrides	*Ebudae Insulae*
Hexham	*Axelodunum*
Ilkley	*Olicana*
Ireland	*Hibernia*

Jersey	*Caesarea*
Kent	*Cantium*
Lanchester	*Longovicium*
Land's End	*Bolerium Promunturium*
Leicester	*Ratae Corieltauvorum*
Lincoln	*Lindum*
Lizard Point	*Damnonium Promunturium*
London	*Londinium*
Manchester	*Mamucium*
Man, Isle of	*Monapia*
Newcastle upon Tyne	*Pons Aelius*
Orkneys	*Orcades*
Pevensey	*Anderetium*
Portsmouth	*Magnus Portus*
Richborough	*Rutupiae*
Rochester	*Durobrivae*
St Albans	*Verulamium*
Salisbury (Old Sarum)	*Sorviodunum*
Scilly Isles	*Cassiterides*
Scotland	*Caledonia*
Severn, R.	*Sabrina*
Silchester	*Calleva Atrebatum*
Solway Firth	*Ituna aestuarium*
Thames, R.	*Tamesis*
Wales	*Cambria*
Wallsend	*Segedunum*
Wash, The	*Metaris aestuarium*
Wear, R.	*Vedra*
Wight, Isle of	*Vectis*
Winchester	*Venta Belgarum*
Worcester	*Vigornia*
Wroxeter	*Viroconium Cornoviorum*
York	*Eburacum*

CONTINENTS

Africa	*Libya, Africa*
Europe	*Europa*

COUNTRIES AND REGIONS

Belgium	*Belgae*
Brittany	*Armoricae*
China	*Seres*
Denmark	*Dania*
Egypt	*Aegyptus*
Flanders	*Menapii*
France	*Gallia*
Gaul	*Gallia*

Germany	*Germania*
Gibraltar	*Calpe*
Greece	*Graecia*
Holland	*Batavi*
Italy	*Italia*
Lebanon	*Libanus*
Malta	*Melita*
Morocco	*Mauretania*
Portugal	*Lusitania*
Spain	*Hispania*
Switzerland	*Helvetia*
Tuscany	*Etruria*

SEAS AND RIVERS

Atlantic Ocean	*Mare Atlanticum*
Black Sea	*Pontus (Euxinus)*
Caspian Sea	*Mare Caspium*
Dardanelles	*Hellespontus*
Gibraltar, Straits of	*Fretum Gaditanum*
Marmora, Sea of	*Propontis*
Mediterranean	*Mare internum*
Nile, R.	*Nilus*
Persian Gulf	*Mare Rubrum*
Red Sea	*Sinus Arabicus*
Rhine, R.	*Rhenus*
Tyrrhenian Sea	*Mare Inferum*

CITIES

Berlin	*Berolinum*
Berne	*Verona*
Cadiz	*Gades*
Constantinople	*Byzantium*
Istanbul	*Byzantium*
Jerusalem	*Hierosolyma*
Lisbon	*Olisipo*
Paris	*Lutetia*

THE CINQUE PORTS

As their name implies, the Cinque Ports were originally five in number: Hastings, New Romney, Hythe, Dover and Sandwich. They were formed during the 11th century to defend the Channel coast and, after the Norman Conquest, were recognized as a Confederation by a charter of 1278. The 'antient towns' of Winchelsea and Rye were added at some time after the Conquest. The other members of the Confederation, known as Limbs, are Lydd, Faversham, Folkestone, Deal, Tenterden, Margate and Ramsgate.

Until 1855 the duty of the Cinque Ports was to provide ships and men for the defence of the state in return for considerable privileges, such as tax exemptions and the framing of by-laws. Of these privileges only jurisdiction in Admiralty remains.

The Barons of the Cinque Ports have the ancient privilege of attending the Coronation ceremony and are allotted special places in Westminster Abbey.

LORD WARDENS OF THE CINQUE PORTS SINCE 1904

Year appointed	
1904	The Marquess Curzon
1905	The Prince of Wales
1908	The Earl Brassey
1913	The Earl Beauchamp
1934	The Marquess of Reading
1936	The Marquess of Willingdon
1941	Winston Churchill
1965	Sir Robert Menzies
1978	HM Queen Elizabeth the Queen Mother

TIME

TIME ZONES

Standard time differences from the Greenwich meridian
+ hours ahead of GMT
- hours behind GMT
* may vary from standard time at some part of the year (Summer Time or Daylight Saving Time)

	Hours	Min
Afghanistan	+ 4	30
Albania★	+ 1	
Algeria	+ 1	
Andorra★	+ 1	
Angola	+ 1	
Anguilla	– 4	
Antigua and Barbuda	– 4	
Argentina	– 3	
Armenia★	+ 4	
Aruba	– 4	
Ascension Island	0	
Australia★	+10	
Broken Hill area (NSW)★	+ 9	30
Lord Howe Island★	+10	30
Northern Territory	+ 9	30
South Australia★	+ 9	30
Western Australia	+ 8	
Austria★	+ 1	
Azerbaijan★	+ 4	
Azores★	– 1	
Bahamas★	– 5	
Bahrain	+ 3	
Bangladesh	+ 6	
Barbados	– 4	
Belarus★	+ 2	
Belgium★	+ 1	
Belize	– 6	
Benin	+ 1	
Bermuda★	– 4	
Bhutan	+ 6	
Bolivia	– 4	
Bosnia-Hercegovina★	+ 1	
Botswana	+ 2	
Brazil		
Acre	– 5	
central states	– 4	
N. and NE coastal states	– 3	
S. and E. coastal states, including Brasilia★	– 3	
Fernando de Noronha Island	– 2	
western	– 5	

	Hours	Min
British Antarctic Territory	– 3	
British Indian Ocean Territory	+ 5	
Diego Garcia	+ 6	
British Virgin Islands	– 4	
Brunei	+ 8	
Bulgaria★	+ 2	
Burkina Faso	0	
Burundi	+ 2	
Cambodia	+ 7	
Cameroon	+ 1	
Canada		
Alberta★	– 7	
British Columbia★	– 8	
Labrador★	– 4	
Manitoba★	– 6	
New Brunswick★	– 4	
Newfoundland★	– 3	30
Northwest Territories★		
east of 85°W.	– 5	
85°W.–102°W.	– 6	
west of 102°W.	– 7	
Nova Scotia★	– 4	
Ontario★		
east of 90° W.	– 5	
west of 90° W.	– 6	
Prince Edward Island★	– 4	
Quebec		
east of 63° W.	– 4	
west of 63° W.★	– 5	
Saskatchewan	– 6	
Yukon★	– 8	
Canary Islands★	0	
Cape Verde	– 1	
Cayman Islands	– 5	
Central African Republic	+ 1	
Chad	+ 1	
Chatham Islands★	+12	45
Chile★	– 4	
China	+ 8	
Christmas Island (Indian Ocean)	+ 7	
Cocos Keeling Islands	+ 6	30
Colombia	– 5	
Comoros	+ 3	
Congo (Dem. Rep.)		
west	+ 1	
Congo (Rep. of)	+ 1	
Cook Islands	–10	

	Hours	*Min*
Costa Rica	- 6	
Côte d'Ivoire	0	
Croatia★	+ 1	
Cuba★	- 5	
Cyprus★	+ 2	
Czech Republic★	+ 1	
Denmark★	+ 1	
Djibouti	+ 3	
Dominica	- 4	
Dominican Republic	- 4	
Ecuador	- 5	
Galápagos Islands	- 6	
Egypt★	+ 2	
El Salvador	- 6	
Equatorial Guinea	+ 1	
Eritrea	+ 3	
Estonia★	+ 2	
Ethiopia	+ 3	
Falkland Islands★	- 4	
Faröe Islands★	0	
Fiji	+12	
Finland★	+ 2	
France★	+ 1	
French Guiana	- 3	
French Polynesia	-10	
Marquesas Islands	- 9	30
Gabon	+ 1	
The Gambia	0	
Georgia	+ 3	
Germany★	+ 1	
Ghana	0	
Gibraltar★	+ 1	
Greece★	+ 2	
Greenland★	- 3	
Danmarkshavn	0	
Mesters Vig	0	
Scoresby Sound★	- 1	
Thule area★	- 4	
Grenada	- 4	
Guadeloupe	- 4	
Guam	+10	
Guatemala	- 6	
Guinea	0	
Guinea-Bissau	0	
Guyana	- 4	
Haiti★	- 5	
Honduras	- 6	
Hungary★	+ 1	

	Hours	Min
Iceland	0	
India	+ 5	30
Indonesia		
Bali	+ 8	
Flores	+ 8	
Irian Jaya	+ 9	
Java	+ 7	
Kalimantan (south and east)	+ 8	
Kalimantan (west and central)	+ 7	
Molucca Islands	+ 9	
Sulawesi	+ 8	
Sumatra	+ 7	
Sumbawa	+ 8	
Tanimbar	+ 9	
Timor	+ 8	
Iran★	+ 3	30
Iraq★	+ 3	
Ireland, Republic of★	0	
Israel★	+ 2	
Italy★	1 1	
Jamaica	− 5	
Japan	+ 9	
Jordan★	+ 2	
Kazakhstan★		
western (Aktau)	+ 4	
central (Atyrau)	+ 5	
eastern	+ 6	
Kenya	+ 3	
Kiribati	+12	
Line Islands	+14	
Phoenix Islands	+13	
Korea, North	+ 9	
Korea, South	+ 9	
Kuwait	+ 3	
Kyrgyzstan★	+ 5	
Laos	+ 7	
Latvia★	+ 2	
Lebanon★	+ 2	
Lesotho	+ 2	
Liberia	0	
Libya★	+ 2	
Liechtenstein★	+ 1	
Line Islands not part of Kiribati	−10	
Lithuania★	+ 1	
Luxembourg★	+ 1	
Macao	+ 8	
Macedonia (Former Yug. Rep. of)★	+ 1	

	Hours	Min
Macedonia (Former Yug. Rep. of)★	+ 1	
Madagascar	+ 3	
Madeira★	0	
Malawi	+ 2	
Malaysia	+ 8	
Maldives	+ 5	
Mali	0	
Malta★	+ 1	
Marshall Islands	+12	
Ebon Atoll	–12	
Martinique	– 4	
Mauritania	0	
Mauritius	+ 4	
Mexico★	– 6	
Nayarit, Sinaloa, Sonora, S. Baga California	– 7	
N. Baga California	– 8	
Micronesia		
Caroline Islands	+10	
Kosrae	+11	
Pingelap	+11	
Pohnpei	+11	
Moldova★	+ 2	
Monaco★	+ 1	
Mongolia★	+ 8	
Montserrat	– 4	
Morocco	0	
Mozambique	+ 2	
Myanmar	+ 6	30
Namibia★	+ 1	
Nauru	+12	
Nepal	+ 5	45
Netherlands★	+ 1	
Netherlands Antilles	– 4	
New Caledonia	+11	
New Zealand★	+12	
Nicaragua	– 6	
Niger	+ 1	
Nigeria	+ 1	
Niue	–11	
Norfolk Island	+11	30
Northern Mariana Islands	+10	
Norway★	+ 1	
Oman	+ 4	
Pakistan	+ 5	
Palau	+ 9	
Panama	– 5	
Papua New Guinea	+10	

	Hours	Min
Paraguay★	– 4	
Peru	– 5	
Philippines	+ 8	
Poland★	+ 1	
Portugal★	0	
Puerto Rico	– 4	
Qatar	+ 3	
Réunion	+ 4	
Romania★	+ 2	
Russia★		
Zone 1	+ 2	
Zone 2	+ 3	
Zone 3	+ 4	
Zone 4	+ 5	
Zone 5	+ 6	
Zone 6	+ 7	
Zone 7	+ 8	
Zone 8	+ 9	
Zone 9	+10	
Zone 10	+11	
Zone 11	+12	
Rwanda	+ 2	
St Helena	0	
St Christopher and Nevis	– 4	
St Lucia	– 4	
St Pierre and Miquelon★	– 3	
St Vincent and the Grenadines	– 4	
Samoa	–11	
Samoa, American	–11	
San Marino★	+ 1	
São Tomé and Príncipe	0	
Saudi Arabia	+ 3	
Senegal	0	
Seychelles	+ 4	
Sierra Leone	0	
Singapore	+ 8	
Slovakia★	+ 1	
Slovenia★	+ 1	
Solomon Islands	+11	
Somalia	+ 3	
South Africa	+ 2	
South Georgia	– 2	
Spain★	+ 1	
Sri Lanka	+ 6	
Sudan	+ 2	
Suriname	– 3	

	Hours	*Min*
Swaziland	+ 2	
Sweden★	+ 1	
Switzerland★	+ 1	
Syria★	+ 2	
Taiwan	+ 8	
Tajikistan	+ 5	
Tanzania	+ 3	
Thailand	+ 7	
Togo	0	
Tonga	+13	
Trinidad and Tobago	- 4	
Tristan da Cunha	0	
Tunisia	+ 1	
Turkey★	+ 2	
Turkmenistan	+ 5	
Turks and Caicos Islands★	- 5	
Tuvalu	+12	
Uganda	+ 3	
Ukraine★	+ 2	
United Arab Emirates	+ 4	
United Kingdom★	0	
United States★		
Alaska	- 9	
Aleutian Islands, east of 169°30′;W.	- 9	
Aleutian Islands, west of 169°30′;W.	-10	
eastern time	- 5	
central time	- 6	
Hawaii	-10	
mountain time	- 7	
Pacific time	- 8	
Uruguay	- 3	
Uzbekistan	+ 5	
Vanuatu	+11	
Vatican City State★	+ 1	
Venezuela	- 4	
Vietnam	+ 7	
Virgin Islands (US)	- 4	
Yemen	+ 3	
Yugoslavia (Fed. Rep. of)★	+ 1	
Zambia	+ 2	
Zimbabwe	+ 2	

TIME MEASUREMENT

Measurements of time are based on the time taken:
    by the Earth to rotate on its axis (day)
    by the Moon to revolve around the Earth (month)
    by the Earth to revolve around the Sun from equinox to
    equinox (year)
The orbits on which these time-scales are based are not uniform
so average or mean periods have been adopted for everyday use.

Period	Actual length	Mean length
Day	23 hours, 56 minutes, 4 seconds	24 hours, each of 60 minutes
Month (from New Moon to New)	29 days, 12 hours, 44 minutes	varies from 28 to 31 days
Year (tropical)	365 days, 5 hours, 48 minutes, 45 seconds	365 days (366 in leap years), each of 24 hours

LEAP YEARS

The tropical year (the period of the Earth's orbit around the Sun)
is 365 days 6 hours minus about 11 minutes 15 seconds. Because
of the difference between the length of the tropical year and the
mean year used for calendar purposes, the natural time-scale and
the calendar get out of step by 11 minutes 15 seconds each year.
The growing difference between the two is corrected by having a
leap year every four years.

   However, a leap year brings the calendar back by 45 minutes
too much. To correct this, the last year of a century is in most
cases not a leap year, but the omission corrects the calendar by six
hours too much; compensation for this is made by every fourth
end-century year being a leap year.

   A year is a leap year if the date of the year is divisible by four
without remainder, unless it is the last year of the century. The last
year of the century is a leap year if the date of the year is divisible
by 400 without remainder, e.g. the years 1800 and 1900 were not
leap years but the year 2000 will be a leap year.

THE SEASONS

Because the Earth's axis is tilted at 66.5° to the plane in which it
orbits the Sun, each hemisphere alternately leans towards or away
from the Sun, causing the seasons. The seasons are defined as:

Season	Astronomical definition	Popular definition
Spring	vernal equinox to summer solstice	March, April, May

Summer	summer solstice to autumnal equinox	June, July, August
Autumn	autumnal equinox to winter solstice	September, October, November
Winter	winter solstice to vernal equinox	December, January, February

THE SOLSTICE

A solstice is the point in the tropical year at which the Sun is at its greatest distance north or south of the Equator. In the northern hemisphere, the furthest point north is the summer solstice (longest day) and the furthest point south is the winter solstice (shortest day).

| Summer solstice | 21 June in 2000 |
| Winter solstice | 21 December in 2000 |

THE EQUINOX

The equinox is the point at which the Sun crosses the Equator and day and night are of equal length all over the world. This occurs around 20 or 21 March (vernal equinox) and 22 or 23 September (autumnal equinox).

CALENDARS

The year-numbering system and the calendar now used more or less world-wide are those of western Europe, i.e. the Christian chronology and Gregorian calendar.

CHRISTIAN CHRONOLOGY

The Christian era is numbered from the birth of Christ. Years after the birth of Christ are denoted by AD (*Anno Domini* – In the Year of Our Lord). Years before the birth of Christ are denoted by the letters BC (Before Christ) or, more rarely, AC (*Ante Christum*). The actual date of the birth of Christ is uncertain.

The system was introduced into Italy in the sixth century. Though first used in France in the seventh century, it did not become universally used there until the eighth century. The system was reputedly introduced into England by St Augustine in the sixth century, but it was not generally used until the Council of Chelsea (AD 816) ordered its use.

THE GREGORIAN CALENDAR

The Gregorian calendar is based on the Julian calendar adopted in the Roman Republic in 45 BC at the instigation of Julius Caesar (see Roman Calendar, below). The Julian calendar had a year of 365 days, with a leap year of 366 days every four years, including the last year of each century.

Because the end-century years in the Julian calendar were leap years, by the end of the 16th century there was a difference of ten days between the tropical year and the calendar year; the vernal equinox fell on 11 March. In 1582 Pope Gregory ordained that 5 October should be called 15 October and that of the end-century years only the fourth should be a leap year.

NAMES OF THE DAYS

The names of the days are derived from Old English translations or adaptations of the Roman names of the Sun, Moon and five planets:

Day	Old English derivation	Roman name
Sunday	Sun	Sol
Monday	Moon	Luna
Tuesday	Tiw/Tyr (god of war)	Mars
Wednesday	Woden/Odin	Mercury
Thursday	Thor	Jupiter
Friday	Frigga/Freyja (goddess of love)	Venus
Saturday	Saeternes	Saturn

NAMES OF THE MONTHS

The names of the months are derived from the pre-Julian Roman calendar, which originally had a year of ten months, beginning with March. Two months, January and February, were subsequently added to make a year of 12 months.

Month	Derivation
January	*Janus*, god of the portal, facing two ways, past and future
February	*Februa*, the Roman festival of purification
March	*Mars*, god of battle
April	*Aperire*, to open; the Earth opens to receive seed
May	*Maia*, goddess of growth and increase
June	*Junius*, the Roman gens (family)
July	the emperor *Julius* Caesar (originally Quintilis, the fifth month)
August	the emperor *Augustus* (originally Sextilis, the sixth month)

Month	*Derivation*
September	*Septem*, the seventh month (of the original Roman calendar)
October	*Octo*, the eighth month
November	*Novem*, the ninth month
December	*Decem*, the tenth month

RELIGIOUS CALENDARS

CHRISTIAN

The Roman Catholic and Protestant Churches use the Gregorian calendar. The church year begins with the first Sunday in the season of Advent and its principal seasons are:

Advent	preparation for Christmas
Christmas	celebration of the birth of Jesus Christ
Epiphany	celebration of the manifestation of Jesus Christ
Lent	preparation for Easter
Easter	celebration of the death and resurrection of Jesus Christ

The principal feasts and holy days in the Church of England are:

Christmas Day	25 December
The Epiphany	6 January
Presentation of Christ in the Temple	2 February
Ash Wednesday	first day of Lent, 40 days before Easter Day
Annunciation to the Blessed Virgin Mary	25 March
Maundy Thursday	Thursday before Easter Day
Good Friday	Friday before Easter Day
Easter Day	date varies according to the Moon
Ascension Day	40 days after Easter Day
Pentecost (Whit Sunday)	nine days after Ascension Day
Trinity Sunday	Sunday after Pentecost
All Saints' Day	1 November

Easter Day can fall at the earliest on 22 March and at the latest on 25 April.

The Eastern Orthodox Churches

Some of the Eastern Orthodox Churches use the Julian calendar and some a modified version of the Julian calendar. The Orthodox church year begins on 1 September. There are four fast periods and, in addition to Pascha (Easter) 12 great feasts, as well as commemorations of the saints of the Old and New Testaments throughout the year.

HINDU

The Hindu calendar is a luni-solar calendar of 12 months, each containing 29 days 12 hours. Each month is divided into a light fortnight (Shukla or Shuddha) and a dark fortnight (Krishna or Vadya) based on the waxing and waning of the Moon. A leap month occurs about every 32 lunar months, whenever the difference between the Hindu year of 360 lunar days (354 days 8 hours solar time) and the 365 days 6 hours of the solar year reaches the length of one Hindu lunar month (29 days 12 hours).

The names of the days of the week are derived from the Sanskrit names of the Sun, the Moon and the planets Mars, Mercury, Jupiter, Venus and Saturn. The months have Sanskrit names derived from 12 asterisms (constellations).

The days are: Raviwar, Somawar, Mangalwar, Budhawar, Guruwar, Shukrawar and Shaniwar. The months are: Chaitra, Vaishakh, Jyeshtha, Ashadh, Shravan, Bhadrapad, Ashvin, Kartik, Margashirsh, Paush, Magh and Phalgun.

The major festivals are:

Chaitra	New Year
Dasara★	victory of Rama over the demon army
Diwali★	festival of lights
Durga-puja★	dedicated to the goddess Durga
Ganesh Chaturthi★	worship of Ganesh
Holi★	spring festival
Janmashtami★	birth festival of the god Krishna
Makara Sankranti	winter solstice festival
Navaratri★	nine-night festival dedicated to the goddess Parvati
Raksha-bandhan★	renewal of kinship bond between brothers and sisters
Ramanavami★	birth festival of the god Rama
Sarasvati-puja★	dedicated to the goddess Sarasvati
Shivatatri	dedicated to the god Shiva

★ The main festivals celebrated by Hindus in the UK

JEWISH

The epoch, or starting point, of Jewish chronology corresponds to 7 October 3761 BC. The calendar is luni-solar; the hour is divided into 1080 minims and the period between one New Moon and the next is reckoned as 29 days 12 hours 793 minims.

The Jewish day begins between sunset and nightfall. The time used is that of the meridian of Jerusalem, which is 2 hours 21 minutes in advance of GMT. Rules for the beginning of sabbaths and festivals were laid down for the latitude of London in the 18th century; hours for nightfall are now fixed annually by the Chief Rabbi.

A Jewish year is one of six types:

Minimal Common	353 days
Regular Common	354 days
Full Common	355 days
Minimal Leap	383 days
Regular Leap	384 days
Full Leap	385 days

Regular year	alternate months of 30 and 29 days
Full year	the second month has 30 instead of 29 days
Minimal year	the third month has 29 instead of 30 days
Leap year	an additional month of 30 days (Adar I) precedes the month of Adar, which in leap years also has 30 days

The months are: Tishri (30 days), Marcheshvan (29/30), Kislev (30/29), Tebet (29), Shebat (30), Adar (29), Nisan (30), Iyar (29), Sivan (30), Tammuz (29), Ab (30), and Elul (29).

The main festivals are:

Rosh Hashanah	New Year
Fast of Gedaliah	
Yom Kippur	Day of Atonement
Succoth	Feast of Tabernacles
Hoshana Rabba	
Shemini Atseret	Solemn Assembly
Simchat Torah	Rejoicing of the Law
Chanucah	Dedication of the Temple
Fast of Tebet	
Fast of Esther	
Purim	Festival of Lots
Shusham Purim	
Pesach	Passover
Shavuot	Feast of Weeks
Fast of Tammuz	
Fast of Ab	

MUSLIM

The Muslim era is dated from the Hijrah, or flight of the Prophet Muhammad from Mecca to Medina; the date corresponds to 16 July AD 622. The calendar is based on a lunar year of about 354 days, consisting of 12 months containing alternate months of 30 and 29 days. A leap day is added at the end of the 12th month at stated intervals in each cycle of 30 years. The purpose of the leap day is to reconcile the date of the first day of the month with the date of the actual New Moon. In each cycle of 30 years, 19 years are common (354 days) and 11 years are leap (kabisah) years (355 days).

Some Muslims still take the date of the evening of the first physical sighting of the crescent of the New Moon as that of the first of the month. If cloud obscures the Moon the present month may be extended to 30 days, after which the new month will begin automatically regardless of whether the Moon has been seen.

The months are: Muharram (30 days), Safar (29), Rabi' I (30), Rabi' II (29), Jumada I (30), Jumada II (29), Rajab (30), Sha'ban (29), Ramadan (30), Shawwâl (29), Dhû'l-Qa'da (30), and Dhû'l-Hijjah (29).

The main festivals are:

Id al-Fitr	marks the end of Ramadan
Id al-Adha	celebrates the submission of the Prophet Ibrahim (Abraham) to God
Ashura	the day Prophet Noah left the Ark and Prophet Moses was saved from Pharaoh (Sunni)
	death of the Prophet's grandson Husain (Shi'ite)
Mawlid al-Nabi	birthday of the Prophet Muhammad
Laylat al-Isra' wa'l-Mi'raj	Night of Journey and Ascension
Laylat al-Qadr	Night of Power

SIKH

The Sikh calendar is a lunar calendar of 365 days divided into 12 months. The length of the months varies between 29 and 32 days.

The main celebrations are:

Baisakhi Mela	New Year
Diwali Mela	festival of light
Hola Mohalla Mela	spring festival (in the Punjab)
the Gurpurbs	anniversaries associated with the ten Gurus

OTHER CALENDARS

CHINESE CALENDAR

Although the Gregorian calendar is used in China for business
and official purposes, the ancient luni-solar calendar still plays an
important part in everyday life. The luni-solar calendar has a cycle
of 60 years. The new year begins at the first New Moon after the
Sun enters the sign of Aquarius, i.e. between 21 January and 19
February in the Gregorian calendar.

Each year in the Chinese calendar is associated with one of 12
animals: the rat, the ox, the tiger, the rabbit, the dragon, the snake,
the horse, the goat or sheep, the monkey, the chicken or rooster,
the dog, and the pig. The next few years are:

2000	Year of the Dragon
2001	Year of the Snake
2002	Year of the Horse
2003	Year of the Goat or Sheep
2004	Year of the Monkey
2005	Year of the Chicken

CHINESE DYNASTIES AND PERIODS

During the imperial period, the numeration of years was based
on a complicated system of reign-titles and other important
events. The main periods and dynasties in Chinese history are:

Date	*Period/Dynasty*
	PRE–IMPERIAL CHINA
*c.*21st–16th century BC	Xia
*c.*16th–11th century BC	Shang
*c.*11th century–770 BC	Western Zhou
770–221 BC	Eastern Zhou
	(Spring and Autumn and
	Warring States periods)
	EARLY EMPIRE
221–207 BC	Qin
206 BC–AD 24	Western Han
25–220	Eastern Han
220–265	Three Kingdoms
	(Wei, Shu and Wu)
265–316	Western Jin
	MIDDLE EMPIRE
317–420	Eastern Jin
420–589	Southern and Northern
	Dynasties
581–618	Sui
618–907	Tang

Date	Period/Dynasty
907–960	Five Dynasties
960–1127	Northern Song
1127–1279	Southern Song
	LATE EMPIRE
1271–1368	Yuan
1368–1644	Ming
1644–1911	Qing
	POST–IMPERIAL CHINA
1912–49	Republic
1949–	People's Republic

JAPANESE CALENDAR

The Japanese calendar is essentially the same as the Gregorian calendar, the years, months and days being of the same length and beginning on the same days.

The numeration of years is different, based on a system of reign-titles, each of which begins at the accession of a new emperor or other important event. The three latest epochs are defined by the reigns of emperors, whose actual names are not necessarily used:

Reign-title	Duration
Taisho	1 August 1912 to 25 December 1926
Showa	26 December 1926 to 7 January 1989
Heisei	8 January 1989

Each year of the epoch begins on 1 January and ends on 31 December.

The months are known as First Month, Second Month, etc., First Month being equivalent to January. The days of the week are:

Nichiyōbi	Sun-day
Getsuyōbi	Moon-day
Kayōbi	Fire-day
Suiyōbi	Water-day
Mokuyōbi	Wood-day
Kinyōbi	Metal-day
Doyōbi	Earth-day

ROMAN CALENDAR

In 46 BC Julius Caesar found that the calendar had fallen into some confusion. He sought the help of the Egyptian astronomer Sosigenes, which led to the construction and adoption in 45 BC of the Julian calendar.

In the Roman (Julian) calendar, the days of the month were counted backwards from three fixed points, or days: the Kalends, the Nones and the Ides. The Kalends was the first day of each month; the Nones fell on the 5th or 7th day; and the Ides on the 13th or 15th day, depending on the month. For example, the Ides of March was on the 15th day of the month and the days preceding the 15th were known as the seventh day before the Ides, the sixth day before the Ides, the fifth day before the Ides, etc.

The Julian calendar included an extra day in every fourth year. A year containing 366 days was called bissextillis annus because it had a doubled sixth day (bissextus dies) before the Kalends of March, i.e. on 24 February.

FRENCH REVOLUTIONARY CALENDAR

The French Revolutionary or Republican calendar was introduced in 1793. It took as its starting point 22 September 1792, the foundation of the first Republic. It was abolished in 1806 on Napoleon's orders.

The year was divided into 12 months, each of 30 days, with five or six extra days at the end. The beginning of the year was the autumnal equinox and the names of the months were intended to reflect the changes of the seasons and the activities of the agricultural year.

Vendémiaire (month of
  grape harvest)   23 September–22 October

NUMBER OF DAYS TABLE

The table shows the number of days from any day in one month to

	Jan	Feb	Mar	April	May	June
January	365	31	59	90	120	151
February	334	365	28	59	89	120
March	306	337	365	31	61	92
April	275	306	334	365	30	61
May	245	276	304	335	365	31
June	214	245	273	304	334	365
July	184	215	243	274	304	335
August	153	184	212	243	273	304
September	122	153	181	212	242	273
October	92	123	151	182	212	243
November	61	92	120	151	181	212
December	31	62	90	121	151	182

Brumaire (month of mist)	23 October–21 November
Frimaire (month of frost)	22 November–21 December
Nivôse (month of snow)	22 December–20 January
Pluviôse (month of rain)	21 January–19 February
Ventôse (month of wind)	20 February–21 March
Germinal (month of buds)	22 March–20 April
Floréal (month of flowers)	21 April–20 May
Prairial (month of meadows)	21 May–19 June
Messidor (month of harvest)	20 June–19 July
Thermidor (month of heat)	20 July–18 August
Fructidor (month of fruit)	19 August–22 September

WEDDING ANNIVERSARIES

1st Cotton
2nd Paper
3rd Leather
4th Fruit and Flower
5th Wood
6th Sugar, or Iron
7th Wool
8th Bronze, or Electrical
    Appliances
9th Copper, or Pottery
10th Tin
11th Steel
12th Silk and Fine Linen

13th Lace
14th Ivory
15th Crystal
20th China
25th Silver
30th Pearl
35th Coral
40th Ruby
45th Sapphire
50th Gold
55th Emerald
60th Diamond
70th Platinum

the same day in any other month of the year (except a leap year).

July	Aug	Sept	Oct	Nov	Dec
181	212	243	273	304	334
150	181	212	242	273	303
122	153	184	214	245	275
91	122	153	183	214	244
61	92	123	153	184	214
30	61	92	122	153	183
365	31	62	92	123	153
334	365	31	61	92	122
303	334	365	30	61	91
273	304	335	365	31	61
242	273	304	334	365	30
212	243	274	304	335	365

SIGNS OF THE ZODIAC

In astronomy, the zodiac is an imaginary belt in the heavens within which lie the apparent paths of the Sun, Moon and major planets. It is bounded by two parallels generally taken as lying 8° on either side of the ecliptic or path of the Sun in its annual course. The zodiac is divided into 12 equal areas, each of 30°.

In astrology, the 12 signs of the zodiac take their names from certain of the constellations with which they once coincided; due to precession, the signs no longer coincide with the constellations whose names they bear but astrology uses the original dates. The dates can vary slightly from year to year according to the day and hour of the Sun's transition from one sign to another; the dates given below are approximate. The signs are considered to begin at the vernal equinox with Aries.

Sign	Symbol	Dates
Aries	the Ram	21 March – 19 April
Taurus	the Bull	20 April – 20 May
Gemini	the Twins	21 May – 21 June
Cancer	the Crab	22 June – 22 July
Leo	the Lion	23 July – 22 August
Virgo	the Virgin	23 August – 22 September
Libra	the Balance	23 September – 23 October
Scorpio	the Scorpion	24 October – 21 November
Sagittarius	the Archer	22 November – 21 December
Capricorn	the Goat	22 December – 19 January
Aquarius	the Water Carrier	20 January – 18 February
Pisces	the Fishes	19 February – 20 March

A 13th sign is used by some astrologers: Ophiuchus, the Serpent Bearer, the second half of Scorpio.

WATCHES ON BOARD SHIP

The crew on board ship is divided into two groups, who keep alternate watches. A watch lasts four hours, except that the time between 4p.m. and 8p.m. is divided into two watches (the first and second dog watches) so that the same men are not always on duty during the same hours each day.

Afternoon watch	noon–4p.m.
First dog watch	4p.m.–6p.m.
Second dog watch	6p.m.–8p.m.
First watch	8p.m.–midnight
Middle watch	midnight–4a.m.
Morning watch	4a.m.–8a.m.
Forenoon watch	8a.m.–noon

PRAYER TIMES

MONASTIC OFFICES

Originally fixed by St Benedict, the history of the Offices is complicated, but normal practice today is as follows:

Vigils/Matins	early morning (6/6.30 a.m.)	
Lauds/Morning Prayer	7.30/8 a.m. *or* immediately after Vigils	
Midday Office	noon *or* Terce	9 a.m.
	Sext	noon
	None	3 p.m.
Vespers	evening prayers (5.30/6/7 p.m.)	
Compline	before retiring for the night	

The time between the end of Compline and the start of Vigils is known as The Great Silence.

ISLAMIC PRAYERS

Salat	Formal prayers to be said at dawn, noon, late afternoon, sunset and night.

SCIENCE

THE SOLAR SYSTEM

	Mean distance from Sun km 10⁶	Period of rotation on axis days
Sun	—	25–35★
PLANETS		
Mercury	58	58.646
Venus	108	243.019r
Earth	150	0.997
Mars	228	1.026
Jupiter	778	0.410e
Saturn	1,427	0.426e
Uranus	2,870	0.718r
Neptune	4,497	0.671
Pluto	5,954	6.387

★ depending on latitude
r retrograde
e equatorial

SATELLITES OF THE PLANETS

	Mean distance from planet km	Period of revolution round planet days
EARTH		
Moon	384,400	27.322
MARS		
Phobos	9,378	0.319
Deimos	23,459	1.262
JUPITER		
Metis	127,960	0.295
Adrastea	128,980	0.298
Amalthea	181,300	0.498
Thebe	221,900	0.675
Io	421,600	1.769
Europa	670,900	3.551
Ganymede	1,070,000	7.155
Callisto	1,883,000	16.689
Leda	11,094,000	239
Himalia	11,480,000	251

	km	*days*
Lysithea	11,720,000	259
Elara	11,737,000	260
Ananke	21,200,000	631r
Carme	22,600,000	692r
Pasiphae	23,500,000	735r
Sinope	23,700,000	758r

SATURN

Pan	133,583	0.575
Atlas	137,670	0.602
Prometheus	139,353	0.613
Pandora	141,700	0.629
Epimetheus	151,422	0.694
Janus	151,472	0.695
Mimas	185,520	0.942
Enceladus	238,020	1.370
Tethys	294,660	1.888
Telesto	294,660	1.888
Calypso	294,660	1.888
Dione	377,400	2.737
Helene	377,400	2.737
Rhea	527,040	4.518
Titan	1,221,830	15.945
Hyperion	1,481,100	21.277
Iapetus	3,561,300	79.330
Phoebe	12,952,000	550.48r

URANUS

Cordelia	49,770	0.335
Ophelia	53,790	0.376
Bianca	59,170	0.435
Cressida	61,780	0.464
Desdemona	62,680	0.474
Juliet	64,350	0.493
Portia	66,090	0.513
Rosalind	69,940	0.558
Belinda	75,260	0.624
Puck	86,010	0.762
Miranda	129,390	1.413
Ariel	191,020	2.520
Umbriel	266,300	4.144
Titania	435,910	8.706
Oberon	583,520	13.463
S/1997 U1	72,000,000	579
S/1997 U2	122,000,000	1,289

NEPTUNE

Naiad	48,230	0.294
Thalassa	50,070	0.311
Despina	52,530	0.335
Galatea	61,950	0.429
Larissa	73,550	0.555
Proteus	117,650	1.122
Triton	354,760	5.877
Nereid	5,513,400	360.136

PLUTO

Charon	19,600	6.387

r retrograde

SI UNITS

The Système International d'Unités (SI) is an international and coherent system of units devised to meet all known needs for measurement in science and technology; it was adopted in 1960.

The system consists of seven base units and the derived units formed as products or quotients of various powers of the base units.

BASE UNITS

metre (m) = unit of length
kilogram (kg) = unit of mass
second (s) = unit of time
ampere (A) = unit of electric current
kelvin (K) = unit of thermodynamic temperature
mole (mol) = unit of amount of substance
candela (cd) = unit of luminous intensity

DERIVED UNITS

hertz (Hz) = unit of frequency
newton (N) = unit of force
pascal (Pa) = unit of pressure, stress
joule (J) = unit of energy, work, quantity of heat
watt (W) = unit of power, radiant flux
coulomb (C) = unit of electric charge, quantity of
  electricity
volt (V) = unit of electric potential, potential difference,
  electromotive force
farad (F) = unit of electric capacitance

ohm (Ω) = unit of electric resistance
siemens (S) = unit of electric conductance
weber (Wb) = unit of magnetic flux
tesla (T) = unit of magnetic flux density
henry (H) = unit of inductance
degree Celsius (°C) = unit of Celsius temperature
lumen (lm) = unit of luminous flux
lux (lx) = unit of illuminance
becquerel (Bq) = unit of activity (of a radionuclide)
gray (Gy) = unit of absorbed dose, specific energy imparted, kerma, absorbed dose index
sievert (Sv) = unit of dose equivalent, dose equivalent index
radian (rad) = unit of plane angle
steradian (sr) = unit of solid angle

OTHER DERIVED UNITS

Other derived units are expressed in terms of base units. Some of the more commonly-used are:
Unit of area = square metre (m^2)
Unit of volume = cubic metre (m^3)
Unit of velocity = metre per second ($m\ s^{-1}$)
Unit of acceleration = metre per second squared ($m\ s^{-2}$)
Unit of density = kilogram per cubic metre ($kg\ m^{-3}$)
Unit of momentum = kilogram metre per second ($kg\ m\ s^{-1}$)
Unit of magnetic field strength = ampere per metre ($A\ m^{-1}$)
Unit of surface tension = newton per metre ($N\ m^{-1}$)
Unit of dynamic viscosity = pascal second ($Pa\ s$)
Unit of heat capacity = joule per kelvin ($J\ K^{-1}$)
Unit of specific heat capacity = joule per kilogram kelvin ($J\ kg^{-1}\ K^{-1}$)
Unit of heat flux density, irradiance = watt per square metre ($W\ m^{-2}$)
Unit of thermal conductivity = watt per metre kelvin ($W\ m^{-1}\ K^{-1}$)
Unit of electric field strength = volt per metre ($V\ m^{-1}$)
Unit of luminance = candela per square metre ($cd\ m^{-2}$)

SI PREFIXES

Decimal multiples and submultiples of the SI units are indicated by SI prefixes. These are as follows:

MULTIPLES

yotta (Y) x 10^{24}
zetta (Z) x 10^{21}
exa (E) x 10^{18}
peta (P) x 10^{15}
tera (T) x 10^{12}
giga (G) x 10^{9}
mega (M) x 10^{6}
kilo (k) x 10^{3}

hecto (h) x 10^2
deca (da) x 10

SUBMULTIPLES
deci (d) x 10^{-1}
centi (c) x 10^{-2}
milli (m) x 10^{-3}
micro (i) x 10^{-6}
nano (n) x 10^{-9}
pico (p) x 10^{-12}
femto (f) x 10^{-15}
atto (a) x 10^{-18}
zepto (z) x 10^{-21}
yocto (y) x 10^{-24}

PHYSICS

DEFINITIONS AND LAWS

Acceleration (symbol: *a*): the rate of change of velocity (a vector quantity). SI unit: metre per second squared.

$$\frac{\text{change in velocity}}{\text{time taken for this change}} \quad \text{metres/seconds}^2 \quad (\text{m s}^{-2})$$

Archimedes' principle (Greek mathematician, 287–212 BC): a body that is partially or totally immersed in a fluid is buoyed up by a force that is equal to the weight of the fluid displaced by the body.

Density (symbol: ρ): mass divided by volume (a physical quantity). SI unit: kilogram per cubic metre.

Energy (symbol: *E*): the capacity of a body or system to do work (a physical quantity). SI unit: joule.

Force (symbol *F*): that which causes a body to change its state at rest or linear motion (a vector quantity). The magnitude of the force is equal to the product *ma* where
    m = mass of the body.
    a = acceleration imparted by the force.

Gravitation (Newton's law of): the force of attraction between two given bodies in the universe is directly proportional to the product of their masses and inversely proportional to the square of the distance between them.

Inertia: see Newton's first law of motion.

Mass (symbol: *m*): measures a body's inertia and determines the mutual gravitational attraction between it and another body. SI unit: kilogram. Mass is the amount of 'stuff' in the body. Mass does not depend on gravitational attraction.

Momentum (symbol: *p*): the product of mass and velocity (a physical and vector quantity). SI unit: kilogram metre per second.

Newton's laws of motion (Sir Isaac Newton, 1642–1727)
1 A body will remain in a state of rest or travel in a straight line at constant speed unless acted upon by an external force, i.e. inertia.
2 The rate of change of momentum of a moving body is proportional to and in the same direction as the force acting on it.
3 To every action there is always an equal and opposite reaction.

Power (symbol *P*): the rate of doing work or of heat transfer (a physical quantity). SI unit: watt (1 watt = 1 joule per second).

$$\text{average power} = \frac{\text{work done}}{\text{time taken}} = \frac{\text{energy change}}{\text{time taken}}$$

Pressure (symbol: *p*): the force acting per unit surface area, expressed as

$$\text{pressure} = \frac{\text{force}}{\text{area}}$$

SI unit: pascal (Pa).

Atmospheric pressure is still quoted in millibars. The standard atmospheric pressure at 1013 millibars (Mb) is 1 kilogram cm^{-2}. NB: tyre pressures are still quoted in lb/sq.in. or, more recently, Bar, e.g. 2 Bar.

Relativity, theory of: mass and energy are related by the equation $E = mc^2$, where E is the energy produced by a mass change m, and c is the speed of light.

Scalar: a physical quantity that has magnitude but not direction, e.g. mass. (*see also* vector).

Speed (symbol: *v* or *u*): the rate of change of distance travelled (a scalar quantity). SI unit: metre per second.

$$\text{average speed} = \frac{\text{distance moved}}{\text{time taken}} \text{ m s}^{-1}$$

Time (symbol: *t*): a fundamental physical quantity indicating duration or precise moment. SI unit: second.

Vector: a physical quantity that has magnitude and direction, e.g. acceleration.

Velocity (symbol *v* or *c*): the rate of change of displacement (a vector quantity). SI unit: metre per second.

$$\text{average velocity} = \frac{\text{distance moved in a particular direction}}{\text{time taken}} \text{ m s}^{-1}$$

Weight (symbol: *W*): the gravitational force exerted on a body at a planet's surface, giving it an acceleration equal to the acceleration of free fall, *g*. It should not be confused with mass (*m*): $W = mg$, and therefore varies as *g* varies. (SI unit: newton, although it is measured in units of mass in everyday usage.)

Work (symbol: *W*): a physical quantity expressed as
    force x distance (*Fs*)
where the point of application of a force moves through a distance in the direction of the force. SI unit: joule.

CONSTANTS
GRAVITY
Acceleration of gravity (standard value of acceleration of free fall) (symbol: g_n): 9.806 65 m s^{-2}. The acceleration of gravity varies in different places on the Earth's surface. At Greenwich: 9.81 m/s^2.

Gravitational constant (symbol: G): 6.672 59 x 10^{-11} N m^2 kg^{-2}.

LIGHT
Speed of light in a vacuum (symbol: c): 299 792 458 m s^{-1}.

SOUND
Speed of sound (symbol: c): 331.4 m s^{-1} (in dry air at 0°C).

WAVES
A wave is a periodic vibration in space or in a substance. Waves can be grouped in two ways according to:
1 whether or not they result in a transfer of energy from one place to another:
Travelling (or progressive) wave: the vibrations travel, transferring energy from one place to another, e.g. the waves on the sea
Stationary (or standing) wave: the wave shape remains stationary, rather than moving, and energy is not transferred

2   whether or not the individual points on the wave move in the
    same direction as the wave itself:

Longitudinal wave: particles move in the same direction as the wave
travel, e.g. in a slinky spring

Transverse wave: particles move in a perpendicular direction to the
direction of wave travel, e.g. in water waves

PROPERTIES OF WAVES

Amplitude

Amplitude is the maximum displacement of a wave from the
equilibrium position

Wavelength

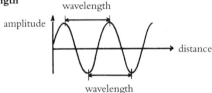

Wavelength is the distance between two successive points along a
wave with similar amplitudes

Period

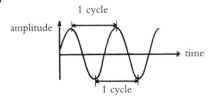

The period of a wave is the time taken for one complete cycle.
Frequency = cycles per second. SI unit: hertz (Hz).
1 cycle per second = 1 hertz

Wave Attenuation

distance

A wave is said to be attenuated when its amplitude becomes progressively reduced as a result of energy loss when it travels through a medium

CHEMISTRY

STATES OF MATTER

The three states of matter are: solid, liquid and gas. When heated,
a solid melts to form a liquid. Melting (or freezing) point is the
temperature above which a solid becomes a liquid. Heating a
liquid to its boiling point causes it to boil and form a gas or
vapour.

Property	Solid	Liquid	Gas
Volume	Definite	Definite	Variable – expands or contracts to fill container
Shape	Definite	Takes up shape of bottom of container	Takes up shape of whole container
Density	High	Medium	Low
Expansion when heated	Low	Medium	High
Effect of applied pressure	Very slight	Slight decrease in volume	Large decrease in volume
Movement of particles	Very slow	Medium	Fast

ELEMENTS AND COMPOUNDS

ELEMENTS

An element is a pure substance that cannot be split up by
chemical reaction. There are 92 known to occur naturally on
earth, and more which have been synthesised under laboratory
conditions. Most that occur naturally are solid and metallic at
room temperature and pressure, although there are exceptions,
e.g. mercury is a liquid and oxygen is a gas.

COMPOUNDS

Some mixtures of elements react together, usually when heated,
to form compounds. These compounds have very different
properties from the elements of which they are composed, e.g.
the gases hydrogen and oxygen combine to form water (H_2O).

NAMING COMPOUNDS

Compounds with the prefix **per–** contain extra oxygen
Compounds with the prefix **thio–** contain a sulphur atom in
place of an oxygen atom
Compounds that end in **–ide** contain two elements
Compounds that end in **–ate** or **–ite** contain oxygen

FORMULAE OF SOME COMMON COMPOUNDS

Compound	Formula
Ammonia	NH_3
Carbon dioxide	CO_2
Carbon monoxide	CO
Hydrogen chloride	HCl
Methane	CH_4
Nitrogen dioxide	NO_2
Sulphur dioxide	SO_2
Sulphur trioxide	SO_3
Water	H_2O
Table salt	$Na\,Cl$

CARBON

Carbon can combine with other elements, notably oxygen, nitrogen and hydrogen, to form the large molecules of which living things are made, e.g., carbohydrates, fats and proteins.

METALS AND ALLOYS

Metals consist of a close-packed, regular arrangement of positive ions surrounded by electrons that hold the ions together (see below). With a few exceptions, they are efficient conductors of heat and electricity, and are both malleable (can be beaten into thin sheets) and ductile (can be extruded into wire). Metals are often combined to form alloys, common examples including:

Alloy	Constituent elements
Brass	Copper and zinc
Bronze	Copper and tin
Duralumin	Aluminium, magnesium, copper and manganese
Solder	Tin and lead
Steel	Iron and carbon, although other metals may be present, e.g. chromium in stainless steel

ATOMIC STRUCTURE

All elements are made up of atoms. An atom is the smallest unit of an element, and atoms of different elements are made up of different combinations of three basic particles: protons, electrons and neutrons. Protons have a positive charge, electrons have a negative charge and neutrons have no charge.

In an atom, the protons and neutrons are tightly packed in the nucleus, while the electrons move rapidly around the outside. The atomic number of an atom is the number of protons it contains, and the mass number is the total number of protons and neutrons.

Atoms contain the same number of protons as electrons, which means that individual atoms have no overall charge. However, an ion is an electrically charged atom or group of atoms formed by the addition or loss of one or more electrons.

ATOMIC BONDING

When atoms join they are said to bond. Several types of bonding occur in common chemicals.

Ionic (or electrovalent) bonding: involves a complete transfer of electrons from one atom to another.

Covalent bonding: involves the sharing of electrons rather than complete transfer.

Metallic bonding: occurs only in metals.

CHEMICAL GROUPS

Elements can be divided into groups, which include the following.

THE ALKALI METAL GROUP

This is a group of very reactive metals, the most common of which are Lithium (Li), Sodium (Na) and Potassium (K).

THE HALOGEN GROUP

This is a group of non-metals, all of which are different in appearance but have similar chemical reactions. They include: Fluorine (F), Chlorine (Cl), Bromine (Br) and Iodine (I).

THE NOBLE (OR INERT) GAS GROUP

As their name suggests, these gases are unreactive:

Helium (He)
Neon (Ne)
Argon (Ar)
Krypton (Kr)
Xenon (Xe)
Radon (Rn)

THE PERIODIC TABLE

The periodic table is a table of chemical elements arranged in order of increasing proton number. The elements are grouped into seven rows or 'periods', and elements in the vertical columns or 'groups' have similar properties (see above).

The elements listed in the periodic table are given below, but in alphabetical rather than atomic number order. The atomic mass is given for each element; an asterisk indicates where the relative atomic mass given is that of the isotope with the longest known half-life.

Element	Symbol	Atomic no.	Atomic mass
Actinium	Ac	89	227.03*
Aluminium	Al	13	26.98
Americium	Am	95	243.06*
Antimony	Sb	51	121.76
Argon	Ar	18	39.95
Arsenic	As	33	74.92
Astatine	At	85	210.00*
Barium	Ba	56	137.33
Berkelium	Bk	97	247.07*
Beryllium	Be	4	9.01
Bismuth	Bi	83	208.98
Bohrium	Bh	107	264.12*
Boron	B	5	10.81
Bromine	Br	35	79.90
Cadmium	Cd	48	112.41
Caesium	Cs	55	132.91
Calcium	Ca	20	40.08
Californium	Cf	98	251.08*
Carbon	C	6	12.01
Cerium	Ce	58	140.12
Chlorine	Cl	17	35.45
Chromium	Cr	24	52.00
Cobalt	Co	27	58.93
Copper	Cu	29	63.55
Curium	Cm	96	247.07*
Dubnium	Db	104	261.11*
Dysprosium	Dy	66	162.50*
Einsteinium	Es	99	252.08*
Erbium	Er	68	167.26
Europium	Eu	63	151.96
Fermium	Fm	100	257.10*
Fluorine	F	9	19.00
Francium	Fr	87	223.02*
Gadolinium	Gd	64	157.25
Gallium	Ga	31	69.72

Element	Symbol	Atomic no.	Atomic mass
Germanium	Ge	32	72.61
Gold	Au	79	196.97
Hafnium	Hf	72	178.49
Hahnium	Hn	108	265.13★
Helium	He	2	4.00
Holmium	Ho	67	164.93
Hydrogen	H	1	1.01
Indium	In	49	114.82
Iodine	I	53	126.90
Iridium	Ir	77	192.22
Iron	Fe	26	55.85
Joliotium	Jl	105	262.11★
Krypton	Kr	36	83.80
Lanthanum	La	57	138.91
Lawrencium	Lr	103	262.11★
Lead	Pb	82	207.20
Lithium	Li	3	6.94
Lutetium	Lu	71	174.97
Magnesium	Mg	12	24.31
Manganese	Mn	25	54.94
Meitnerium	Mt	109	268.00★
Mendelevium	Md	101	258.10★
Mercury	Hg	80	200.59
Molybdenum	Mo	42	95.94
Neodymium	Nd	60	144.24
Neon	Ne	10	20.18
Neptunium	Np	93	237.05★
Nickel	Ni	28	58.69
Niobium	Nb	41	92.91
Nitrogen	N	7	14.00
Nobelium	No	102	259.10★
Osmium	Os	76	190.23
Oxygen	O	8	16.00
Palladium	Pd	46	106.42
Phosphorus	P	15	30.97
Platinum	Pt	78	195.08
Plutonium	Pu	94	244.06★
Polonium	Po	84	208.98★
Potassium	K	19	39.10
Praseodymium	Pr	59	140.91★
Promethium	Pm	61	144.91★
Protactinium	Pa	91	231.04
Radium	Ra	88	226.03★
Radon	Rn	86	222.02★
Rhenium	Re	75	186.21
Rhodium	Rh	45	102.91
Rubidium	Rb	37	85.47
Ruthenium	Ru	44	101.07

Element	Symbol	Atomic no.	Atomic mass
Rutherfordium	Rf	106	266.12★
Samarium	Sm	62	150.36
Scandium	Sc	21	44.96
Selenium	Se	34	78.96
Silicon	Si	14	28.09
Silver	Ag	47	107.87
Sodium	Na	11	22.99
Strontium	Sr	38	87.62
Sulphur	S	16	32.07
Tantalum	Ta	73	180.95
Technetium	Tc	43	97.91
Tellurium	Te	52	127.60
Terbium	Tb	65	158.93
Thallium	Tl	81	204.38
Thorium	Th	90	232.04
Thulium	Tm	69	168.93
Tin	Sn	50	118.71
Titanium	Ti	22	47.87
Tungsten (Wolfram)	W	74	183.84
Ununnilium	Uuu	110	271.00★
Unununium	Uun	111	272.00★
Uranium	U	92	238.03
Vanadium	V	23	50.94
Xenon	Xe	54	131.29
Ytterbium	Yb	70	173.04
Yttrium	Y	39	88.91
Zinc	Zn	30	65.39
Zirconium	Zr	40	91.22

THE PH SCALE

The pH of a substance is a measure of its alkalinity or acidity. A pH reading below 7 indicates an acid solution while readings above 7 indicate an alkaline solution.

```
0
1
2
3          Acid
4
5
6
7        Neutral
8
9
10
11       Alkaline
12
13
14
```

Litmus paper shows whether a solution is acidic or alkaline: blue indicates an alkali and red an acid. It is possible to obtain special paper that gives an approximate measure of pH by colour change. For very accurate measurements a pH meter must be used.

pH VALUES OF BODY FLUIDS

Blood	7.4–7.5
Saliva	6.4–7.4
Urine	5.7
Sweat	4–6.8
Breast milk	7.0
Stomach contents	varies but approx. 2

CIRCULATION OF MATERIALS

There is a constant interchange between the materials of living
things and the environment, i.e. the air, soil and sea. Plants absorb
carbon dioxide (CO_2) from the air for photosynthesis to make
carbohydrates. Plants and animals release CO_2 when they respire.
Oxygen is released by plants during photosynthesis and used by
nearly all organisms for respiration.

Simple nitrogen compounds (e.g. nitrates) are absorbed by plant
roots and used to build proteins. This nitrogen returns to the soil
when living things die and decay. The supply of available nitrogen
is also increased by nitrogen-fixing soil bacteria and lightning.

Most water absorbed from the soil passes straight through the
plant and evaporates (transpiration); some is retained for
photosynthesis but eventually returned via respiration. This
balance can be upset by man's activities such as excessive
deforestation and the burning of fossil fuels.

THE CARBON CYCLE

THE CARBON CYCLE

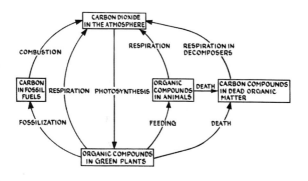

THE NITROGEN CYCLE

THE CARBON CYCLE

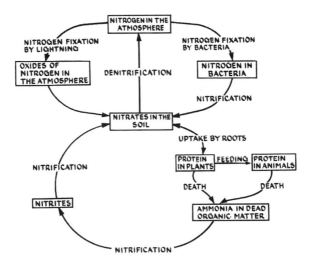

PHOTOSYNTHESIS (IN GREEN PLANTS)

(requires light energy)

carbon dioxide and water ⟶ sugar + oxygen

RESPIRATION (IN MOST PLANT AND ANIMAL CELLS)

Sugar + oxygen ⟶ carbon dioxide + water
(releases energy)

LIFE SCIENCES

GENETICS AND EVOLUTION

Most cells have a nucleus containing a fixed number of
chromosomes, half derived from each parent. The chromosomes
carry genetic (inherited) information along their lengths as genes.
In sexual reproduction the parents' genes are mixed and
recombined so the offspring usually show characteristics of both.

In 1953, Crick and Watson in Cambridge showed that the genes
were short lengths of deoxyribonucleic acid (DNA) and that the
genetic information is contained in just four chemical groups
taken three at a time. A gene is a sequence of these chemical
'words'. DNA is now used in the identification of individuals.

Charles Darwin (1809 - 82) described how the enormous variety
of living things could have evolved through the 'natural selection'
by the environment of those plants and animals best fitted to
survive and reproduce themselves in the harshly competitive
natural world.

CLASSIFICATION OF PLANTS AND ANIMALS

All species of plants and animals are named according to their
genus and their species.

Species: the fundamental unit of biological classification; a group of
organisms capable of breeding to produce fertile offspring. They
are very similar, but do show variety.

Genus: a category of biological classification; a group of organisms
with a large number of similarities but whose different sub-
groups or species are usually unable to interbreed successfully.

All species are named according to the binomial system invented
by Carl Linnaeus in 1735. Under this system the genus name is
written first, with a capital letter, e.g. *Homo* (man). The species
name, which starts with a small letter, is written second, e.g.
sapiens (modern).

GROUPS AND SUB-GROUPS

Just as species are sub-groups of genera, so Linnaeus grouped
genera into larger and larger groups. They are listed as follows,
from the largest (kingdom) to smallest (species):

Kingdom
Phylum (for animals) or Divisions (for plants)
Class
Order
Family
Genus
Species

The Plant Kingdom

The plant kingdom is divided into the following divisions, some of which are further sub-divided into two or more classes:

Divisions	*Classes*
Algae	
Bacteria	
Bryophyta	Musci (mosses)
	Hepaticae (liverworts)
Fungi	
Lichens	
Pteridophyta	Pteropsida (ferns)
	Sphenopsida (horsetails)
	Lycopsida (club-mosses)
Spermatophyta (seed-bearing plants)	Gymnosperms (cone-bearing)
	Angiosperms (flower-bearing, seeds within fruits)

The Animal Kingdom

Invertebrates (no backbones)

Phylum	*Class*
Annelida (segmented worms)	
Arthropoda	Arachnida (spiders)
	Crustacea (hard outer shells)
	Insecta (with a head, thorax and abdomen and 3 pairs of legs)
	Myriapoda (with many legs)
Coelenterata (sac-like body, special sting cells)	
Echinodermata (symmetrical marine animals)	
Mollusca (shell, soft body)	
Nematoda (unsegmented worms)	
Platyhelminthes (flat-bodied worms)	
Protozoa (single celled)	

Vertebrates (with backbones)

Phylum	*Class*
Chordata	Amphibia (living on land and water, can breathe dissolved or atmospheric oxygen)
	Aves (birds, feathred, constant body temperature)
	Mammalia (suckle their young, constant body temperature)
	Pisces (fish, breathe dissolved oxygen)
	Reptilia (scaly, cold-blooded, egg-laying)

PARTS OF A FLOWER

Stamen = the male parts of a flower
Carpel = the female parts of a flower (ovary, stigma)

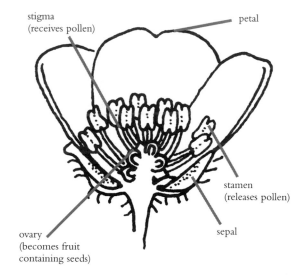

stigma
(receives pollen)

petal

stamen
(releases pollen)

sepal

ovary
(becomes fruit
containing seeds)

THE HUMAN BODY

THE SKELETON — FRONT VIEW

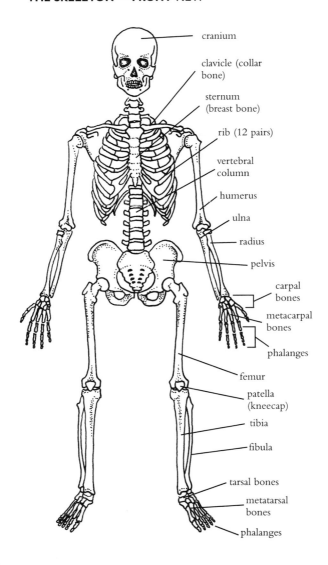

cranium

clavicle (collar bone)

sternum (breast bone)

rib (12 pairs)

vertebral column

humerus

ulna

radius

pelvis

carpal bones

metacarpal bones

phalanges

femur

patella (kneecap)

tibia

fibula

tarsal bones

metatarsal bones

phalanges

THE SKELETON — SIDE VIEW

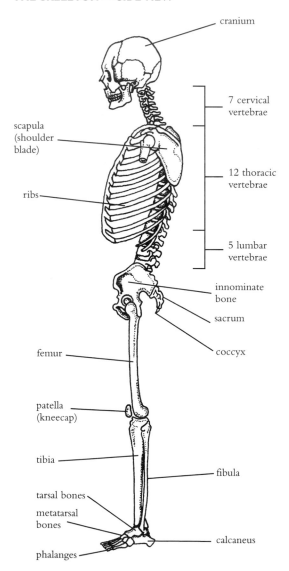

cranium

7 cervical vertebrae

12 thoracic vertebrae

5 lumbar vertebrae

scapula (shoulder blade)

ribs

innominate bone

sacrum

coccyx

femur

patella (kneecap)

tibia

fibula

tarsal bones

metatarsal bones

calcaneus

phalanges

MAIN MUSCLE GROUPS

Muscle group	Body part	Primary functions
abductors (gluteus medius and minimus)	outer thigh	draw hip outwards
adductors	inner thigh	draw hip inwards
anterior tibialis	shin	draws ball of the foot upwards
biceps brachii	upper arm, front	bends elbow swings shoulder joint forward
biceps femoris (hamstrings)	back of thigh	straightens hip bends knee and rotates it outwards
deltoideus	shoulder/ upper arm	involved in all movements of upper arm
erector spinae	lower back	straightens spine
gastrocnemius	calf	bends knee straightens ankle (points toes)
gluteus maximus	buttocks	straightens hip rotates thigh outwards
iliopsoas (psoas major, iliacus)	hip	bends hip rotates leg outwards
latissimus dorsi (broad back muscle)	back	draws arm backwards
obliques (internal and external)	waist	rotate torso bend torso to side
pectoralis major (greater chest muscle)	chest	draws arm inwards pulls arm in front of chest from any position
quadriceps femoris (rectus femoris, vastus medialis, intermedialis, lateralis)	thigh	straightens knee bends hip
rectus abdominus	stomach	bends spine forwards
sartorius (tailor's muscle)	thigh	bends and rotates hip outwards bends and rotates knee inwards (lets you sit cross-legged)
soleus (flounder muscle)	lower calf	standing on toes

Muscle group	Body part	Primary functions
trapezius	neck and upper back	draws shoulder blades back
		turns head
		bends neck backwards
triceps brachii	upper arm, back	straightens elbow

PERIODS OF GESTATION OR INCUBATION

The table shows approximate periods of gestation or incubation for some common animals and birds; in some cases the periods may vary.

Species	Shortest period (days)	Usual period (days)	Longest period (days)
Human	240	273	313
Horse	305	336	340
Cow	273	280	294
Goat	147	151	155
Sheep	140	147–50	160
Pig	109	112	125
Dog	55	63	70
Cat	53	56	63
Rabbit	30	32	35
Goose	28	30	32
Turkey	25	28	28
Duck	28	28	32
Chicken	20	21	22
Pigeon	17	18	19
Canary	12	14	14
Guinea Pig	63	—	70
Rat	21	—	24
Mouse	18	—	19
Elephant		21–22 months	
Zebra		56 weeks	
Camel		45 weeks	

MATHEMATICS

NUMBERS

Binary numbers: the binary system, or binary notation, uses only the binary digits 0 and 1 to represent any number. It is said to have base 2; the more usual decimal system, using all 10 digits from 0 to 9, has a base of 10. Binary notation is the number system most commonly used in computers since the two numerals correspond to the on and off positions of an electronic switch. Counting in the binary system is: 1, 10 (=2+0), 11(=2+1), 100 (=4+0+0), 101 (=4+0+1), etc.

Binary numbers from 1 to 20 with their decimal equivalents:

1	1	11	1011
2	10	12	1100
3	11	13	1101
4	100	14	1110
5	101	15	1111
6	110	16	10000
7	111	17	10001
8	1000	18	10010
9	1001	19	10011
10	1010	20	10100

To decipher binary numbers, remember the following rules:
— ignore all noughts in the calculation
— count the right column as 1
— count the second column on the right as 2
— count the third column on the right as 4
— count the fourth column on the right as 8
— count the fifth column on the right as 16, and so on.

Cube root: see Cubic number.

Cubic number: the product of multiplying a whole number by itself, and then the product of that by the whole number again, e.g. 3 x 3 x 3 = 27. Therefore 3 is the *cube root* of 27.

Difference: the result when one number is subtracted from another.

Even number: a whole number that divides by 2 exactly, i.e. to give a whole number without leaving a remainder.

Factor: a whole number that divides into another number without leaving a remainder.

Fibonacci numbers (Leonardo Fibonacci, *c*.1170–*c*.1250): beginning 1, 1, a series of numbers in which each number is the sum of the two numbers preceding it, e.g. 1, 1, 2 (1 + 1), 3 (1 + 2), 5 (2 + 3), 8 (3 + 5), 13, 21, 34, 55 etc. This sequence appears in nature, e.g. as the number of petals on the rim of a sunflower, the pattern of scales on a pine cone and the spiral shape of a nautilus shell.

Fraction: see below.

Highest common factor (HCF): the largest number that divides into two or more numbers without leaving a remainder is the HCF of the numbers.

Index: a number placed above the line after another number to show how many times the number on the line is to be multiplied by itself (e.g. 4^2). The value of the index is called the *power*.

Integer: any positive or negative whole number, including zero.

Irrational number: a number that cannot be expressed as a fraction or ratio of integers.

Lowest common multiple (LCM): the smallest number that divides by two or more numbers without leaving a remainder is the LCM of the numbers.

Modulus (of a number): its magnitude, ignoring sign, e.g. the modulus of both 3 and -3 is 3.

Multiple: a number that is the product of a given number and any other integer.

Natural (or whole) number: a number that is a positive integer.

Odd number: an integer that will not divide by 2 without leaving a remainder.

Perfect number: a number that is equal to the sum of its factors, excluding the number itself. Only 30 have been discovered so far, the first of which is 6:
>   factors of 6 (excluding 6 itself) = 1,2 and 3
>   1 + 2 + 3 = 6

Power: see Index.

Prime number: with the exception of 1, any natural number that can only be divided by itself and 1.

Prime numbers between 1 and 1000

2	3	5	7	11	13	17
19	23	29	31	37	41	43
47	53	59	61	67	71	73
79	83	89	97	101	103	107
109	113	127	131	137	139	149
151	157	163	167	173	179	181
191	193	197	199	211	223	227
229	233	239	241	251	257	263
269	271	277	281	283	293	307
311	313	317	331	337	347	349
353	359	367	373	379	383	389
397	401	409	419	421	431	433
439	443	449	457	461	463	467
479	487	491	499	503	509	521
523	541	547	557	563	569	571
577	587	593	599	601	607	613
617	619	631	641	643	647	653
659	661	673	677	683	691	701
709	719	727	733	739	743	751
757	761	769	773	787	797	809
811	821	823	827	829	839	853
857	859	863	877	881	883	887
907	911	919	929	937	941	947
953	967	971	977	983	991	997

Product: the result of multiplying numbers together.

Quotient: the result of dividing one number by another number. Also referred to as a ratio.

Ratio: see Quotient.

Rational number: any number that can be expressed as a quotient of integers.

Remainder: the amount left over when one number cannot be exactly divided by another.

Square number: the product of multiplying a whole number by itself, e.g. 3 x 3 = 9, Therefore, 3 is the square root of 9.

Square root: see Square number.

Whole number: see natural number

Unity: the number 1

FRACTIONS, DECIMALS AND PERCENTAGES

Fraction: any quantity expressed as a ratio of two numbers, a numerator and a denominator (see below), written one above the other, separated by a line. When the numerator is less than the denominator, the fraction is of magnitude less than unity.

Decimal point: a dot that separates whole numbers from the fractional part in a decimal notation number.

Decimal fraction: a quantity less than unity expressed in decimal notation, e.g. 0.375.

Denominator: the number below the line in a fraction that denotes the number of equal parts into which the numerator is divided.

Improper fraction: a fraction in which the numerator is larger than the denominator, e.g. $^{13}/_{12}$.

Mixed number: a number that comprises an integer and a fraction, e.g. $4^1/_2$ (in other words $4 + {}^1/_2$).

Numerator: the number above the line in a fraction which denotes the number of fractional parts taken.

Recurring (fractions, decimals and percentages): a pattern that repeats indefinitely.

Proper fraction: one in which the numerator is smaller than the denominator, e.g. $^7/_{12}$.

Vulgar fraction (also known as simple and common fraction): a quantity expressed as a fraction with integers as numerator and denominator, as opposed to being expressed as a decimal fraction, e.g. $^1/_4$ rather than 0.25.

CORRESPONDING FRACTIONS, DECIMALS AND PERCENTAGES

These are three different ways of showing the same information:

Fraction	Decimal	Percentage (%)
$^1/_{20}$	0.05	5.00
$^1/_{10}$	0.10	10.00
$^1/_9$	0.11111★	11.11
$^1/_8$	0.125	12.50
$^1/_7$	0.14286	14.28
$^1/_6$	0.16667★	16.67
$^1/_5$	0.20	20.00
$^1/_4$	0.25	25.00
$^1/_3$	0.33333★	33.33

Fraction	Decimal	Percentage
$^1/_2$	0.50	50.00
$^2/_3$	0.66667★	66.66
$^3/_4$	0.75	75.00

★ = recurring; by convention a recurring digit equal to or greater than 5 is rounded up

GEOMETRY AND TRIGONOMETRY

Geometry is the branch of mathematics that deals with the properties of lines, points, surfaces and solids.

Acute angle: an angle of less than 90°, i.e. less than a quarter of a complete rotation.

Cos: *see* Cosine.

Cosine of an angle (abbrev. cos): in a right angle triangle, the ratio of the side adjacent to the given angle to the hypotenuse.

Degree (°): the magnitude of an angle of 1/360 of a complete rotation.
Hypotenuse: the side of a right-angled triangle that is opposite the right angle.

Right angle: a quarter of a complete rotation in angle (90°).

Sin: *see* Sine.

Sine of an angle (abbrev. sin): in a right angle triangle, the ratio of the side opposite the given angle to the hypotenuse.

Tangent of an angle (abbrev. tan): in a right angle triangle, the ratio of the side opposite the given angle to the adjacent side.

Trigonometry: the branch of mathematics that deals with the relations between the sides and angles of triangles.

POLYGONS

A polygon is a closed plane figure with three or more straight sides (usually implies more than four).

Number of sides	Name of polygon
3	triangle
4	quadrilateral
5	pentagon
6	hexagon
7	heptagon

8	octagon
9	nonagon
10	decagon
12	dodecagon

Equilateral triangle: a triangle which has three equal sides; each of its internal angles is 60°.

Isosceles triangle: a triangle in which two of the sides are of equal length.

Parallelogram: a quadrilateral whose opposite sides are parallel and equal in length.

Pythagoras' theorem (Greek mathematician and philosopher, *c*.580–*c*.500 BC): the square drawn on the hypotenuse is equal in size to the sum of the squares drawn on the other two sides.

Rectangle: a rhombus whose vertices are all at right angles.

Rhombus: a parallelogram whose sides are of equal length.

Scalene triangle: a triangle with unequal length sides and no axes of symmetry.

Square: a rectangle with equal length sides.

Trapezium: a quadrilateral with two parallel sides of unequal length.

Vertex (*plural* vertices): the point at which two sides of a polygon meet.

CIRCLES AND OTHER CONIC SECTIONS

Circle: a plane figure bounded by one line, every point on which is an equal distance from a fixed point at the centre.

Arc: any part of the circumference of a circle.

Circumference: the line that forms the complete perimeter of a circle.

Diameter: a straight line that passes through the centre of a circle (or other figure) and terminates at the circumference at each end. The term also describes the length of such a line.

pi (indicated by the Greek letter π): the ratio of the circumference of a circle to its diameter (approximately 3.141592...)

Radius (*plural* radii): a straight line from the circumference of a circle to its centre.

ANGULAR AND CIRCULAR MEASURES

60 seconds (″) = 1 minute (′)
60 minutes = 1 degree (°)
90 degrees = 1 right angle or quadrant
Circumference of circle = diameter (or 2 x radius) x 3.1416, i.e.
   πd or 2πr
Area of circle = radius squared x 3.1416, i.e. πr^2
Surface of sphere = 4 x radius squared x 3.1416, i.e. $4\pi r^2$
Volume of sphere = $^4/_3$ x radius cubed x 0.523, i.e. $^4/_3\,\pi r^3$
Radius$\star$ = one degree of circumference x 57.3, i.e. $360/2\pi$
Curved surface of cylinder = circumference of circular base x
   3.1416 x length or height, i.e. 2πrh
Volume of cylinder = area of circular base x length or height,
i.e. πr^2h

$\star$Or, one radian (the angle subtended at the centre of a circle by an arc of the circumference equal in length to the radius) = 57.3 degrees

MATHEMATICAL SYMBOLS

= Equal to
≠ Not equal to
≈ Approximately equal to
≡ Identically equal to
÷ Divide
x Multiplication
∞ Infinity
∝ Proportional to
∥ Parallel to
⊥ Perpendicular to
≥ Greater than or equal to
≱ Not greater than or equal to
> Greater than
≯ Not greater than
≫ Much greater than
≷ Greater than or less than
≤ Less than or equal to
≰ Not less than or equal to
< Less than
≮ Not less than
≪ Much less than
≶ Less than or greater than
± Plus or minus
∫ Integral sign
√ Square root

$\sqrt[3]{}$ Cube root
$\sqrt[n]{}$ *n*-th root
∂ Partial differentiation
Σ Sum of

ROMAN NUMERALS

1	I	30	XXX
2	II	40	XL
3	III	50	L
4	IV	60	LX
5	V	70	LXX
6	VI	80	LXXX
7	VII	90	XC
8	VIII	100	C
9	IX	200	CC
10	X	300	CCC
11	XI	400	CD
12	XII	500	D
13	XIII	600	DC
14	XIV	700	DCC
15	XV	800	DCCC
16	XVI	900	CM
17	XVII	1000	M
18	XVIII	1500	MD
19	XIX	1900	MCM
20	XX	2000	MM

EXAMPLES

43	XLIII
66	LXVI
98	XCVIII
339	CCCXXXIX
619	DCXIX
988	CMLXXXVIII
996	CMXCVI
1674	MDCLXXIV
1962	MCMLXII
1998	MCMXCVIII

A bar placed over a numeral has the effect of multiplying the
number by 1,000, e.g.

6,000	$\overline{\text{VI}}$
16,000	$\overline{\text{XVI}}$
160,000	$\overline{\text{CLX}}$
666,000	$\overline{\text{DCLXVI}}$

WEIGHTS AND MEASURES

METRIC UNITS

The metric primary standards are the metre as the unit of
measurement of length, and the kilogram as the unit of
measurement of mass. Other units of measurement are defined by
reference to the primary standards.

MEASUREMENT OF LENGTH
Kilometre (km) = 1000 metres
Metre (m) is the length of the path travelled by light in vacuum
    during a time interval of 1/299792458 of a second
Decimetre (dm) = 1/10 metre
Centimetre (cm) = 1/100 metre
Millimetre (mm) = 1/1000 metre

MEASUREMENT OF AREA
Hectare (ha) = 100 ares
Decare = 10 ares
Are (a) = 100 square metres
Square metre = a superficial area equal to that of a square each
    side of which measures one metre
Square decimetre = 1/100 square metre
Square centimetre = 1/100 square decimetre
Square millimetre = 1/100 square centimetre

MEASUREMENT OF VOLUME
Cubic metre (m^3) = a volume equal to that of a cube each edge
    of which measures one metre
Cubic decimetre = 1/1000 cubic metre
Cubic centimetre (cc) = 1/1000 cubic decimetre
Hectolitre = 100 litres
Litre = a cubic decimetre
Decilitre = 1/10 litre
Centilitre = 1/100 litre
Millilitre = 1/1000 litre

MEASUREMENT OF CAPACITY
Hectolitre (hl) = 100 litres
Litre (l or L) = a cubic decimetre
Decilitre (dl) = 1/10 litre
Centilitre (cl) = 1/100 litre
Millilitre (ml) = 1/1000 litre

MEASUREMENT OF MASS OR WEIGHT
Tonne (t) = 1000 kilograms
Kilogram (kg) is equal to the mass of the international prototype
    of the kilogram

Hectogram (hg) = 1/10 kilogram
Gram (g) = 1/1000 kilogram
Carat, metric★ = 1/5 gram
Milligram (mg) = 1/1000 gram

★Used only for transactions in precious stones or pearls

IMPERIAL UNITS

The imperial primary standards are the yard as the unit of
measurement of length and the pound as the unit of
measurement of mass. Other units of measurement are defined by
reference to the primary standards. Most of these units are no
longer authorized for use in trade in the UK – *see* below.

MEASUREMENT OF LENGTH
Mile = 1760 yards
Furlong = 220 yards
Chain = 22 yards
Yard (yd) = 0.9144 metre
Foot (ft) = 1/3 yard
Inch (in) = 1/36 yard

MEASUREMENT OF AREA
Square mile = 640 acres
Acre = 4840 square yards
Rood = 1210 square yards
Square yard (sq. yd) = a superficial area equal to that of a square
    each side of which measures one yard
Square foot (sq. ft) = 1/9 square yard
Square inch (sq. in) = 1/144 square foot

MEASUREMENT OF VOLUME
Cubic yard = a volume equal to that of a cube each edge of
    which measures one yard
Cubic foot = 1/27 cubic yard
Cubic inch = 1/1728 cubic foot

MEASUREMENT OF CAPACITY
Bushel = 8 gallons
Peck = 2 gallons
Gallon (gal) = 4.546 09 cubic decimetres
Quart (qt) = 1/4 gallon
Pint (pt)★ = 1/2 quart
Gill = 1/4 pint
Fluid ounce (fl oz)★ = 1/20 pint
Fluid drachm = 1/8 fluid ounce
Minim (min) = 1/60 fluid drachm

MEASUREMENT OF MASS OR WEIGHT

Ton = 2240 pounds
Hundredweight (cwt) = 112 pounds
Cental = 100 pounds
Quarter = 28 pounds
Stone = 14 pounds
Pound (lb)★ = 0.453 592 37 kilogram
Ounce (oz)★ = 1/16 pound
Ounce troy (oz tr)★† = 12/175 pound
Dram (dr) = 1/16 ounce
Grain (gr) = 1/7000 pound
Pennyweight (dwt) = 24 grains
Ounce apothecaries = 480 grains
★Units of measurement still authorized for use for trade in the UK
†Used only for transactions in gold, silver or other precious metals, and articles made therefrom

METRICATION IN THE UK

Imperial units were replaced by metric units for trade from 30 September 1995, when imperial units ceased to be authorized for use in the UK for economic, public health, public safety and administrative purposes, with the following exceptions:

Units of measurement authorized for use in specialized fields between 1 October 1995 and 31 December 1999:

Unit	Field of application
fathom	Marine navigation
fluid ounce ⌉	Beer, cider, water, lemonade, fruit juice in
pint ⌡	returnable containers
ounce ⌉	
pound ⌡	Goods for sale loose from bulk
therm	Gas supply

Units of measurement authorized for use in specialized fields from 1 October 1995, without time limit:

Unit	Field of application
inch ⌉	Road traffic signs
foot	Distance and speed measurement
yard	
mile ⌡	
pint ⌈	Dispense of draught beer or cider
⌊	Milk in returnable containers
acre	Land registration
troy ounce	Transactions in precious metals

MILLIONS AND BILLIONS

VALUE IN THE UK

Million	thousand x thousand	10^6
Billion★	million x million	10^{12}
Trillion	million x billion	10^{18}
Quadrillion	million x trillion	10^{24}

VALUE IN THE USA

Million	thousand x thousand	10^6
Billion★	thousand x million	10^9
Trillion	million x million	10^{12}
Quadrillion	million x billion US	10^{15}

★The American usage of billion (i.e. 10^9) is increasingly common, and is now universally used by statisticians

PAPER SIZES

A SERIES (MAGAZINES, BOOKS)

	mm		
A0	841	x	1189
A1	594	x	841
A2	420	x	594
A3	297	x	420
A4	210	x	297
A5	148	x	210
A6	105	x	148
A7	74	x	105
A8	52	x	74
A9	37	x	52
A10	26	x	37

B SERIES (POSTERS, WALL CHARTS, OTHER LARGE ITEMS)

	mm		
B0	1000	x	1414
B1	707	x	1000
B2	500	x	707
B3	353	x	500
B4	250	x	353
B5	176	x	250
B6	125	x	176
B7	88	x	125
B8	62	x	88
B9	44	x	62
B10	31	x	44

C and DL Series (envelopes)

	mm		
C4	324	x	229
C5	229	x	162
C6	114	x	162
DL	110	x	220

NAUTICAL MEASURES

DISTANCE

Distance at sea is measured in nautical miles. The British standard nautical mile was 6080 feet but this measure has been obsolete since 1970, when the international nautical mile of 1852 metres was adopted by the Ministry of Defence.

The cable (600 feet or 100 fathoms) was a measure approximately one-tenth of a nautical mile. Such distances are now expressed in decimal parts of a sea mile or in metres.

Soundings at sea were recorded in fathoms (6 feet); depths are now expressed in metres on Admiralty charts.

SPEED

Speed is measured in nautical miles per hour, called knots. A ship moving at the rate of 30 nautical miles per hour is said to be doing 30 knots.

knots	*m.p.h.*
1	1.1515
2	2.3030
3	3.4545
4	4.6060
5	5.7575
6	6.9090
7	8.0606
8	9.2121
9	10.3636
10	11.5151
15	17.2727
20	23.0303
25	28.7878
30	34.5454
35	40.3030
40	46.0606

WATER AND LIQUOR MEASURES

1 litre weighs 1 kg
1 cubic metre weighs 1 tonne
1 gallon weighs 10 lb

WATER FOR SHIPS
Kilderkin = 18 gallons
Barrel = 36 gallons
Puncheon = 72 gallons
Butt = 110 gallons
Tun = 210 gallons

BOTTLES OF WINE
Traditional equivalents in standard champagne bottles:
Magnum = 2 bottles
Jeroboam = 4 bottles
Rehoboam = 6 bottles
Methuselah = 8 bottles
Salmanazar = 12 bottles
Balthazar = 16 bottles
Nebuchadnezzar = 20 bottles

A quarter of a bottle is known as a nip
An eighth of a bottle is known as a baby

TEMPERATURE SCALES

The Fahrenheit scale is related to the Celsius scale by the
relationships:
temperature °F = (temperature °C x 1.8) + 32
temperature °C = (temperature °F –32) divided by 1.8

°C	°F
100	212
95	203
90	194
85	185
80	176
75	167
70	158
65	149
60	140
55	131
50	122
45	113
40	104
35	95
30	86

°C	°F
25	77
20	68
15	59
10	50
5	41
zero	32
–5	23
–10	14
–15	5

The freezing point of water is 0°C and 32°F
The boiling point of water is 99.974°C and 211.953°F
Body temperature varies between 36.5°C and 37.2°C
(97.70–98.9°F)

OVEN TEMPERATURES

Gas Mark	Electric °C	°F
	110	225
	130	250
1	140	275
2	150	300
3	170	325
4	180	350
5	190	375
6	200	400
7	220	425
8	230	450
9	240	475

CONVERSION TABLES

Bold figures equal units of either of the columns beside them;
thus: 1 cm = 0.394 inches and 1 inch = 2.540 cm

LENGTH

Centimetres		Inches
2.540	**1**	0.394
5.080	**2**	0.787
7.620	**3**	1.181
10.160	**4**	1.575
12.700	**5**	1.969
15.240	**6**	2.362
17.780	**7**	2.756
20.320	**8**	3.150
22.860	**9**	3.543

Centimetres		Inches
25.400	10	3.937
50.800	20	7.874
76.200	30	11.811
101.600	40	15.748
127.000	50	19.685
152.400	60	23.622
177.800	70	27.559
203.200	80	31.496
228.600	90	35.433
254.000	100	39.370

Metres		Yards
0.914	1	1.094
1.829	2	2.187
2.743	3	3.281
3.658	4	4.374
4.572	5	5.468
5.486	6	6.562
6.401	7	7.655
7.315	8	8.749
8.230	9	9.843
9.144	10	10.936
18.288	20	21.872
27.432	30	32.808
36.576	40	43.745
45.720	50	54.681
54.864	60	65.617
64.008	70	76.553
73.152	80	87.489
82.296	90	98.425
91.440	100	109.361

Kilometres		Miles
1.609	1	0.621
3.219	2	1.243
4.828	3	1.864
6.437	4	2.485
8.047	5	3.107
9.656	6	3.728
11.265	7	4.350
12.875	8	4.971
14.484	9	5.592
16.093	10	6.214
32.187	20	12.427
48.280	30	18.641
64.374	40	24.855
80.467	50	31.069
96.561	60	37.282

Kilometres		Miles
112.654	**70**	43.496
128.748	**80**	49.710
144.841	**90**	55.923
160.934	**100**	62.137

AREA

Square cm		Square in
6.452	**1**	0.155
12.903	**2**	0.310
19.355	**3**	0.465
25.806	**4**	0.620
32.258	**5**	0.775
38.710	**6**	0.930
45.161	**7**	1.085
51.613	**8**	1.240
58.064	**9**	1.395
64.516	**10**	1.550
129.032	**20**	3.100
193.548	**30**	4.650
258.064	**40**	6.200
322.580	**50**	7.750
387.096	**60**	9.300
451.612	**70**	10.850
516.128	**80**	12.400
580.644	**90**	13.950
645.160	**100**	15.500

Square m		Square yd
0.836	**1**	1.196
1.672	**2**	2.392
2.508	**3**	3.588
3.345	**4**	4.784
4.181	**5**	5.980
5.017	**6**	7.176
5.853	**7**	8.372
6.689	**8**	9.568
7.525	**9**	10.764
8.361	**10**	11.960
16.723	**20**	23.920
25.084	**30**	35.880
33.445	**40**	47.840
41.806	**50**	59.799
50.168	**60**	71.759
58.529	**70**	83.719
66.890	**80**	95.679
75.251	**90**	107.639
83.613	**100**	119.599

Hectares		Acres
0.405	1	2.471
0.809	2	4.942
1.214	3	7.413
1.619	4	9.844
2.023	5	12.355
2.428	6	14.826
2.833	7	17.297
3.327	8	19.769
3.642	9	22.240
4.047	10	24.711
8.094	20	49.421
12.140	30	74.132
16.187	40	98.842
20.234	50	123.555
24.281	60	148.263
28.328	70	172.974
32.375	80	197.684
36.422	90	222.395
40.469	100	247.105

VOLUME

Cubic cm		Cubic in
16.387	1	0.061
32.774	2	0.122
49.161	3	0.183
65.548	4	0.244
81.936	5	0.305
98.323	6	0.366
114.710	7	0.427
131.097	8	0.488
147.484	9	0.549
163.871	10	0.610
327.742	20	1.220
491.613	30	1.831
655.484	40	2.441
819.355	50	3.051
983.226	60	3.661
1147.097	70	4.272
1310.968	80	4.882
1474.839	90	5.492
1638.710	100	6.102

Cubic m		Cubic yd
0.765	1	1.308
1.529	2	2.616
2.294	3	3.924
3.058	4	5.232
3.823	5	6.540

Cubic m		Cubic yd
4.587	**6**	7.848
5.352	**7**	9.156
6.116	**8**	10.464
6.881	**9**	11.772
7.646	**10**	13.080
15.291	**20**	26.159
22.937	**30**	39.239
30.582	**40**	52.318
38.228	**50**	65.398
45.873	**60**	78.477
53.519	**70**	91.557
61.164	**80**	104.636
68.810	**90**	117.716
76.455	**100**	130.795

Litres		Gallons
4.546	**1**	0.220
9.092	**2**	0.440
13.638	**3**	0.660
18.184	**4**	0.880
22.730	**5**	1.100
27.276	**6**	1.320
31.822	**7**	1.540
36.368	**8**	1.760
40.914	**9**	1.980
45.460	**10**	2.200
90.919	**20**	4.400
136.379	**30**	6.599
181.839	**40**	8.799
227.298	**50**	10.999
272.758	**60**	13.199
318.217	**70**	15.398
363.677	**80**	17.598
409.137	**90**	19.798
454.596	**100**	21.998

WEIGHT (MASS)

Kilograms		Pounds
0.454	**1**	2.205
0.907	**2**	4.409
1.361	**3**	6.614
1.814	**4**	8.819
2.268	**5**	11.023
2.722	**6**	13.228
3.175	**7**	15.432
3.629	**8**	17.637
4.082	**9**	19.842
4.536	**10**	22.046
9.072	**20**	44.092

Kilograms		Pounds
13.608	**30**	66.139
18.144	**40**	88.185
22.680	**50**	110.231
27.216	**60**	132.277
31.752	**70**	154.324
36.287	**80**	176.370
40.823	**90**	198.416
45.359	**100**	220.464

Metric tonnes		Tons (UK)
1.016	**1**	0.984
2.032	**2**	1.968
3.048	**3**	2.953
4.064	**4**	3.937
5.080	**5**	4.921
6.096	**6**	5.905
7.112	**7**	6.889
8.128	**8**	7.874
9.144	**9**	8.858
10.161	**10**	9.842
20.321	**20**	19.684
30.481	**30**	29.526
40.642	**40**	39.368
50.802	**50**	49.210
60.963	**60**	59.052
71.123	**70**	68.894
81.284	**80**	78.737
91.444	**90**	88.579
101.605	**100**	98.421

Metric tonnes		Tons (US)
0.907	**1**	1.102
1.814	**2**	2.205
2.722	**3**	3.305
3.629	**4**	4.409
4.536	**5**	5.521
5.443	**6**	6.614
6.350	**7**	7.716
7.257	**8**	8.818
8.165	**9**	9.921
9.072	**10**	11.023
18.144	**20**	22.046
27.216	**30**	33.069
36.287	**40**	44.092
45.359	**50**	55.116
54.431	**60**	66.139
63.503	**70**	77.162

Metric tonnes		Tons (US)
72.575	**80**	88.185
81.647	**90**	99.208
90.719	**100**	110.231

CLOTHING SIZE CONVERSIONS

MEN'S

Item	UK	USA	Europe
Suits	36	36	46
	38	38	48
	40	40	50
	42	42	52
	44	44	54
	46	46	56
Shirts	12	12	30–31
	$12^{1}/_{2}$	$12^{1}/_{2}$	32
	13	13	33
	$13^{1}/_{2}$	$13^{1}/_{2}$	34–35
	14	14	36
	$14^{1}/_{2}$	$14^{1}/_{2}$	37
	15	15	38
	$15^{1}/_{2}$	$15^{1}/_{2}$	39–40
	16	16	41
	$16^{1}/_{2}$	$16^{1}/_{2}$	42
	17	17	43
	$17^{1}/_{2}$	$17^{1}/_{2}$	44–45
Socks	9	9	38–39
	10	10	39–40
	$10^{1}/_{2}$	$10^{1}/_{2}$	40–41
	11	11	41–42
	$11^{1}/_{2}$	$11^{1}/_{2}$	42–43
Shoes	$6^{1}/_{2}$	7	39
	7	$7^{1}/_{2}$	40
	$7^{1}/_{2}$	8	41
	8	$8^{1}/_{2}$	42
	$8^{1}/_{2}$	9	43
	9	$9^{1}/_{2}$	43
	$9^{1}/_{2}$	10	44
	10	$10^{1}/_{2}$	44
	$10^{1}/_{2}$	11	45

WOMEN'S

Item	UK	USA	Europe
Clothing	8	6	36
	10	8	38
	12	10	40

Item	UK	USA	Europe
	14	12	42
	16	14	44
	18	16	46
	20	18	48
	22	20	50
	24	22	52
Shoes	4	5^1/$_2$	37
	4^1/$_2$	6	37
	5	6^1/$_2$	38
	5^1/$_2$	7	38
	6	7^1/$_2$	39
	6^1/$_2$	8	39
	7	8^1/$_2$	40
	7^1/$_2$	9	40
	8	9^1/$_2$	41

MONEY

WORLD CURRENCIES

Country Name	Currency
Afghanistan	Afghani (Af) of 100 puls
Albania	Lek (Lk) of 100 qindarka
Algeria	Algerian dinar (DA) of 100 centimes
American Samoa	Currency is that of the USA
Andorra	French and Spanish currencies in use
Angola	Readjusted kwanza (Kzrl) of 100 lwei
Anguilla	East Caribbean dollar (EC$) of 100 cents
Antigua and Barbuda	East Caribbean dollar (EC$) of 100 cents
Argentina	Peso of 10,000 australes
Armenia	Dram of 100 louma
Aruba	Aruban florin
Ascension Island	Currency is that of St Helena
Australia	Australian dollar ($A) of 100 cents
Norfolk Island	Currency is that of Australia
Austria	Schilling of 100 Groschen
Azerbaijan	Manat of 100 gopik
The Bahamas	Bahamian dollar (B$) of 100 cents
Bahrain	Bahraini dinar (BD) of 1,000 fils
Bangladesh	Taka (Tk) of 100 poisha
Barbados	Barbados dollar (BD$) of 100 cents
Belarus	Rouble of 100 kopeks
Belgium	Belgian franc (or frank) of 100 centimes (centiemen)
Belize	Belize dollar (BZ$) of 100 cents
Benin	Franc CFA
Bermuda	Bermuda dollar of 100 cents
Bhutan	Ngultrum of 100 chetrum (Indian currency is also legal tender)
Bolivia	Boliviano ($b) of 100 centavos
Bosnia-Hercegovina	Convertible marka
Botswana	Pula (P) of 100 thebe
Brazil	Real of 100 centavos
Brunei	Brunei dollar (B$) of 100 sen (fully interchangeable with Singapore currency)
Bulgaria	Lev of 100 stotinki
Burkina Faso	Franc CFA
Burundi	Burundi franc of 100 centimes
Cambodia	Riel of 100 sen
Cameroon	Franc CFA
Canada	Canadian dollar (C$) of 100 cents
Cape Verde	Escudo Caboverdiano of 100 centavos
Cayman Islands	Cayman Islands dollar (CI$) of 100 cents
Central African	Franc CFA

Country Name	*Currency*
Republic	
Chad	Franc CFA
Chile	Chilean peso of 100 centavos
China	Renminbi Yuan of 10 jiao or 100 fen
Hong Kong	Hong Kong dollar (HK$) of 100 cents
Colombia	Colombian peso of 100 centavos
The Comoros	Comorian franc (KMF) of 100 centimes
Congo, Dem. Rep. (formerly Zaïre)	Congolese franc
Congo, Rep. of	Franc CFA
Costa Rica	Costa Rican colón (C) of 100 céntimos
Côte d'Ivoire	Franc CFA
Croatia	Kuna of 100 lipas
Cuba	Cuban peso of 100 centavos
Cyprus	Cyprus pound (C£) of 100 cents
Czech Republic	Koruna (Kčs) of 100 haléřu
Denmark	Danish krone of 100 øre
Faröe Islands	Currency is that of Denmark
Djibouti	Djibouti franc of 100 centimes
Dominica	East Caribbean dollar (EC$) of 100 cents
Dominican Republic	Dominican Republic peso (RD$) of 100 centavos
Ecuador	Sucre of 100 centavos
Egypt	Egyptian pound (£E) of 100 piastres or 1,000 millièmes
El Salvador	El Salvador colón (C) of 100 centavos
Equatorial Guinea	Franc CFA
Eritrea	Nakfa
Estonia	Kroon of 100 sents
Ethiopia	Ethiopian birr (EB) of 100 cents
Falkland Islands	Falkland pound of 100 pence
Fiji	Fiji dollar (F$) of 100 cents
Finland	Markka (Mk) of 100 penniä
France	Franc of 100 centimes
French Guiana	Currency is that of France
French Polynesia	Franc CFP
Gabon	Franc CFA
The Gambia	Dalasi (D) of 100 butut
Georgia	Lari of 100 tetri
Germany	Deutsche Mark (DM) of 100 Pfennig
Ghana	Cedi of 100 pesewas
Gibraltar	Gibraltar pound of 100 pence
Greece	Drachma of 100 leptae
Greenland	Currency is that of Denmark
Grenada	East Caribbean dollar (EC$) of 100 cents
Guadeloupe	Currency is that of France
Guam	Currency is that of USA
Guatemala	Quetzal (Q) of 100 centavos

Country Name	Currency
Guinea	Guinea franc of 100 centimes
Guinea–Bissau	Franc CFA
Guyana	Guyana dollar (G$) of 100 cents
Haiti	Gourde of 100 centimes
Honduras	Lempira of 100 centavos
Hungary	Forint of 100 fillér
Iceland	Icelandic króna (Kr) of 100 aurar
India	Indian rupee (Rs) of 100 paisa
Indonesia	Rupiah (Rp) of 100 sen
Iran	Rial
Iraq	Iraqi dinar (ID) of 1,000 fils
Ireland, Republic of	Punt (IR£) of 100 pence
Israel	Shekel of 100 agora
Italy	Lira of 100 centesimi
Jamaica	Jamaican dollar (J$) of 100 cents
Japan	Yen of 100 sen
Jordan	Jordanian dinar (JD) of 1,000 fils
Kazakhstan	Tenge
Kenya	Kenya shilling (Ksh) of 100 cents
Kiribati	Australian dollar ($A) of 100 cents
Korea, North	Won of 100 chon
Korea, South	Won of 100 jeon
Kuwait	Kuwaiti dinar (KD) of 1,000 fils
Kyrgyzstan	Som
Laos	Kip (K) of 100 at
Latvia	Lats of 100 santimes
Lebanon	Lebanese pound (L£) of 100 piastres
Lesotho	Loti (M) of 100 lisente
Liberia	Liberian dollar (L$) of 100 cents
Libya	Libyan dinar (LD) of 1,000 dirhams
Liechtenstein	Swiss franc of 100 rappen (or centimes)
Lithuania	Litas
Luxembourg	Luxembourg franc (LF) of 100 centimes (Belgian currency is also legal tender)
Macao	Pataca of 100 avos
Macedonia, Former Yugoslav Rep. of	Dinar of 100 paras
Madagascar	Franc malgache (FMG) of 100 centimes
Malawi	Kwacha (K) of 100 tambala
Malaysia	Malaysian dollar (ringgit) (M$) of 100 sen
Maldives	Rufiyaa of 100 laaris
Mali	Franc CFA
Malta	Maltese lira (LM) of 100 cents or 1,000 mils
Marshall Islands	Currency is that of USA
Martinique	Currency is that of France
Mauritania	Ouguiya (UM) of 5 khoums
Mauritius	Mauritius rupee of 100 cents

Country Name	*Currency*
Mayotte	Currency is that of France
Mexico	Peso of 100 centavos
Federated States of Micronesia	Currency is that of USA
Moldova	Leu
Monaco	French franc of 100 centimes
Mongolia	Tugrik of 100 möngö
Montserrat	East Caribbean dollar (EC$) of 100 cents
Morocco	Dirham (DH) of 100 centimes
Mozambique	Metical (MT) of 100 centavos
Myanmar	Kyat (K) of 100 pyas
Namibia	Namibian dollar of 100 cents
Nauru	Australian dollar ($A) of 100 cents
Nepal	Nepalese rupee of 100 paisa
The Netherlands	Gulden (guilder) or florin of 100 cents
Netherlands Antilles	Netherlands Antilles guilder of 100 cents
New Caledonia	Franc CFP
New Zealand	New Zealand dollar (NZ$) of 100 cents
Cook Islands	Currency is that of New Zealand
Niue	Currency is that of New Zealand
Tokelau	Currency is that of New Zealand
Nicaragua	Córdoba (C$) of 100 centavos
Niger	Franc CFA
Nigeria	Naira (N) of 100 kobo
Northern Mariana Islands	Currency is that of USA
Norway	Krone of 100 øre
Oman	Rial Omani (OR) of 1,000 baiza
Pakistan	Pakistan rupee of 100 paisa
Palau	Currency is that of the USA
Panama	Balboa of 100 centésimos (US notes are also in circulation)
Papua New Guinea	Kina (K) of 100 toea
Paraguay	Guaraní (Gs) of 100 céntimos
Peru	New Sol of 100 cénts
The Philippines	Philippine peso (P) of 100 centavos
Pitcairn Islands	Currency is that of New Zealand
Poland	Zloty of 100 groszy
Portugal	Escudo (Esc) of 100 centavos
Puerto Rico	Currency is that of USA
Qatar	Qatar riyal of 100 dirhams
Réunion	Currency is that of France
Romania	Leu (Lei) of 100 bani
Russia	Rouble of 100 kopeks
Rwanda	Rwanda franc of 100 centimes
St Christopher and Nevis	East Caribbean dollar (EC$) of 100 cents

Country Name	Currency
St Helena	St Helena pound (£) of 100 pence
St Lucia	East Caribbean dollar (EC$) of 100 cents
St Pierre and Miquelon	Currency is that of France
St Vincent and The Grenadines	East Caribbean dollar (EC$) of 100 cents
Samoa	Tala (WS$) of 100 sene
San Marino	San Marino and Italian currencies are in circulation
São Tomé and Princípe	Dobra of 100 centavos
Saudi Arabia	Saudi riyal (SR) of 20 qursh or 100 halala
Senegal	Franc CFA
Seychelles	Seychelles rupee of 100 cents
Sierra Leone	Leone (Le) of 100 cents
Singapore	Singapore dollar (S$) of 100 cents
Slovakia	Koruna (Kčs) of 100 haléřu
Slovenia	Tolar (SIT) of 100 stotin
Solomon Islands	Solomon Islands dollar (SI$) of 100 cents
Somalia	Somali shilling of 100 cents
South Africa	Rand (R) of 100 cents
Spain	Peseta of 100 céntimos
Sri Lanka	Sri Lankan rupee of 100 cents
Sudan	Sudanese dinar (SD) of 10 pounds
Suriname	Suriname guilder of 100 cents
Swaziland	Lilangeni (E) of 100 cents (South African currency is also in circulation)
Sweden	Swedish krona of 100 öre
Switzerland	Swiss franc of 100 rappen (or centimes)
Syria	Syrian pound (S$) of 100 piastres
Taiwan	New Taiwan dollar (NT$) of 100 cents
Tajikistan	Tajik rouble (TJR) of 100 tanga
Tanzania	Tanzanian shilling of 100 cents
Thailand	Baht of 100 satang
Togo	Franc CFA
Tonga	Pa'anga (T$) of 100 seniti
Trinidad and Tobago	Trinidad and Tobago dollar (TT$) of 100 cents
Tristan da Cunha	Currency is that of the UK
Tunisia	Tunisian dinar of 1,000 millimes
Turkey	Turkish lira (TL) of 100 kurus
Country Name	Currency
Turkmenistan	Manat
Turks and Caicos Is.	US dollar (US$)
Tuvalu	Australian dollar ($A) of 100 cents
Uganda	Uganda shilling of 100 cents

Country Name	Currency
Ukraine	Hryvna of 100 kopiykas
United Arab Emirates	UAE dirham of 100 fils
United Kingdom	Pound sterling (£) of 100 pence
United States of America	US dollar (US$) of 100 cents
Uruguay	New Uruguayan peso of 100 centésimos
Uzbekistan	Sum
Vanuatu	Vatu of 100 centimes
Vatican City State	Italian currency is legal tender
Venezuela	Bolívar (Bs) of 100 céntimos
Vietnam	Dông of 10 hào or 100 xu
Virgin Islands, British	US dollar (US$) (£ sterling and EC$ also circulate)
Virgin Islands, US	Currency is that of the USA
Wallis and Futuna Islands	Franc CFP
Yemen	Riyal of 100 fils
Yugoslavia	New dinar of 100 paras
Zambia	Kwacha (K) of 100 ngwee
Zimbabwe	Zimbabwe dollar (Z$) of 100 cents

Franc CFA = Franc de la Communauté financière africaine
Franc CFP = Franc des Comptoirs français du Pacifique

BRITISH CURRENCY

The decimal system was introduced on 15 February 1971. The unit of currency is the pound sterling (£) of 100 pence.

COINS

The coins in circulation are:

Denomination	Metal
Penny	bronze
Penny	copper-plated steel
2 pence	bronze
2 pence	copper-plated steel
5 pence	cupro-nickel
10 pence	cupro-nickel
20 pence	cupro-nickel
50 pence	cupro-nickel
£1	nickel-brass
£2	cupro-nickel, nickel-brass

Bronze is an alloy of copper 97 parts, zinc 2.5 parts and tin 0.5 part. These proportions have been subject to slight variations in the past. Bronze was replaced by copper-plated steel in 1992.

Cupro-nickel is an alloy of copper 75 parts and nickel 25 parts, except for the 20p, composed of copper 84 parts, nickel 16 parts.

BANKNOTES

Bank of England notes are currently issued in denominations of £5, £10, £20 and £50.

The current series of notes portray on the back the following prominent figures from British history:

£5	George Stephenson
£10	Charles Dickens
£20	Sir Edward Elgar
£50	Sir John Houblon

LEGAL TENDER

Gold (dated 1838 onwards, if not below least current weight)	to any amount
£5 (Crown since 1990)	to any amount
£2	to any amount
£1	to any amount
50p	up to £10
25p (Crown pre-1990)	up to £10
20p	up to £10
10p	up to £5
5p	up to £5
2p	up to 20p
1p	up to 20p

WITHDRAWN COINS

These coins ceased to be legal tender on the following dates:

Farthing	1960
Halfpenny ($^1/_2$d.)	1969
Half-Crown	1970
Threepence	1971
Penny (1d.)	1971
Sixpence (6d.)	1980
Halfpenny ($^1/_2$p.)	1984
old 5 pence	1990
old 10 pence	1993
old 50 pence	February 1998

The £1 coin was introduced in 1983 to replace the £1 note; no £1 notes have been issued since 1984 and the outstanding £1 notes were written off in March 1998. The 10 shilling note was replaced by the 50p coin in 1969, and ceased to be legal tender in 1970.

MAUNDY MONEY

On Maundy Thursday each year, the Sovereign distributes gifts of special coins (Maundy money) to a number of aged poor men and women corresponding to his or her own age. The Maundy money coins (4p, 3p, 2p, 1p) are the only coins still struck from sterling silver.

PRE-DECIMAL CURRENCY

The pre-decimal unit of currency in the UK was the pound sterling (£ or L.) of 20 shillings (s.) or 240 pennies (d.). L.s.d. was the abbreviation for Librae, solidi, denarii, Latin for pounds, shillings and pence.

Prior to decimalization, the coins in circulation were:

Denomination	Metal
Farthing ($^1/_4$d.)	bronze
Penny (1d.)	bronze
Halfpenny ($^1/_2$d.)	bronze
Threepence (3d.)	nickel-brass (formerly cupro-nickel)
Sixpence (6d.)	cupro-nickel
Shilling (1s.)	cupro-nickel
Florin (2s.)	cupro-nickel
Half-Crown (2s. 6d.)	cupro-nickel

Bank of England notes were issued in denominations of 10s., £1, £5, and £10 at the time of decimalization.

CONVERSION TABLE

Decimal currency	£ s. d.
$^1/_2$p	1d.
1p	2d., 3d.
$1^1/_2$p	4d.
2p	5d.
$2^1/_2$p	6d.
3p	7d.
$3^1/_2$p	8d.
4p	9d., 10d.
$4^1/_2$p	11d.
5p	1s.
10p	2s.

Decimal currency	£ s. d.
12½p	2s.6d.
25p	5s.
50p	10s.
£1	£1

SLANG TERMS FOR MONEY

A joey	4d.
A tanner	6d.
A bob	1s.
Half a bull	2s. 6d.
A bull	5s.
A quid	£1
A pony	£25
A monkey	£500
A plum	£100,000
A kite	an accommodation Bill
Blunt	silver, or money in general
Browns	copper or bronze
Coppers	copper/bronze small denomination coins
Tin	money generally

INLAND LETTER POST RATES

Year	Basic rate	Year	Basic rate
1840	1d	1980	12p
1918	1½ d	1981	14p
1940	2½ d	1982	15½ p
1957	3d	1983	16p
1965	4d	1984	17p
1968★	5d	1986	18p
1971	3p	1988	19p
1973	3½ p	1989	20p
1974	4½ p	1990	22p
1975	7p	1991	24p
1975 Sept	8½ p	1993	25p
1977	9p	1996	26p
1979	10p		

★ Two-tier postal system introduced – subsequent figures are for first class letter post

ALPHABETS AND SYMBOLS

GREEK ALPHABET

		Name of letter	*Trans-literation*
Α	α	alpha	a
Β	β	beta	b
Γ	γ	gamma	g
Δ	δ	delta	d
Ε	ε	epsilon	e
Ζ	ζ	zeta	z
Η	η	eta	ē
Θ	θ	theta	th
Ι	ι	iota	i
Κ	κ	kappa	k
Λ	λ	lambda	l
Μ	μ	mu	m
Ν	ν	nu	n
Ξ	ξ	xi	x
Ο	ο	omicron	o
Π	π	pi	p
Ρ	ρ	rho	r
Σ	σ	sigma	s
Τ	τ	tau	t
Υ	υ	upsilon	u
Φ	φ	phi	ph
Χ	χ	chi	ch
Ψ	ψ	psi	ps
Ω	ω	omega	ō, or Ω

CYRILLIC ALPHABET

		Trans-literation
А	а	a
Б	б	b
В	в	v
Г	г	g
Д	д	d
Е (Ё)	е (ё)	e (ë)
Ж	ж	ž or zh
З	з	z
И	и	i
Й	й	j or ĭ
К	к	k

Л	л	l
М	м	m
Н	н	n
О	о	o
П	п	p
Р	р	r
С	с	s
Т	т	t
У	у	u
Ф	ф	f
Х	х	x or kh
Ц	ц	c or ts
Ч	ч	č or ch
Ш	ш	š or sh
Щ	щ	šč or shch
Ъ	ъ	" or "
Ы	ы	y
Ь	ь	' or '
Э	э	ė or é
Ю	ю	ju or yu
Я	я	ja or ya

ANGLO-SAXON RUNIC ALPHABET

The Anglo-Saxon runic alphabet is known as the Futhorc, from the names of the first six letters.

Rune	Modern letter	Name of rune	Meaning
ᚡ	f	feoh	wealth
ᚢ	u	ur	aurochs
ᚦ	th	þorn	thorn
ᚠ	o	os	mouth
ᚱ	r	rad	riding
ᚳ	c	cen	torch
ᚷ	g	gyfu	gift
ᚹ	w	wynn	joy
ᚻ	h	hægl	hail
ᚾ	n	nyd	need
ᛁ	i	is	ice
ᚵ	j	ger	harvest
ᛇ	eo	eoh	yew
ᛈ	p	peorð	hearth
ᛉ	x	eolhxsecg	elksedge
ᛋ	s	sigel	sun
ᛏ	t	Tir	Tiw

Rune	Modern letter	Name of rune	Meaning
ᛒ	b	beorc	birch
ᛖ	e	eh	horse
ᛗ	m	man	man
ᛚ	l	lagu	water
ᛝ	ng	Ing	Ing
ᛟ	oe	eþel	homeland
ᛞ	d	dæg	day
ᚪ	a	ac	oak
ᚫ	æ	æsc	ash
ᚣ	y	yr	weapon
ᛡ	ia	ior	beaver
ᛠ	ea	ear	grave

INTERNATIONAL RADIO ALPHABET

A	Alfa
B	Bravo
C	Charlie
D	Delta
E	Echo
F	Foxtrot
G	Golf
H	Hotel
I	India
J	Juliet
K	Kilo
L	Lima
M	Mike
N	November
O	Oscar
P	Papa
Q	Quebec
R	Romeo
S	Sierra
T	Tango
U	Uniform
V	Victor
W	Whiskey
X	X-Ray
Y	Yankee
Z	Zulu

MORSE CODE

The International Morse Code was formulated in 1852. The spoken code enables radio operators to send messages with their own voices, using the expressions 'dah' and 'di' or 'dit' instead of keying in dashes and dots on their transmitters.

A	. —	di-dah
B	— . . .	dah-di-di-dit
C	— . — .	dah-di-dah-dit
D	— . .	dah-di-dit
E	.	dit
F	. . — .	di-di-dah-dit
G	— — .	dah-dah-dit
H	. . . .	di-di-di-dit
I	. .	di-dit
J	. — — —	di-dah-dah-dah
K	— . —	dah-di-dah
L	. — . .	di-dah-di-dit
M	— —	dah-dah
N	— .	dah-dit
O	— — —	dah-dah-dah
P	. — — .	di-dah-dah-dit
Q	— — . —	dah-dah-di-dah
R	. — .	di-dah-dit
S	. . .	di-di-dit
T	—	dah
U	. . —	di-di-dah
V	. . . —	di-di-di-dah
W	. — —	di-dah-dah
X	— . . —	dah-di-di-dah
Y	— . — —	dah-di-dah-dah
Z	— — . .	dah-dah-di-dit

Dash = dah
Dot = di or dit

MUSICAL NOTATION

stave, horizontal lines on which the pitch of a
note is indicated

Clef = a sign written at the beginning of the stave to indicate the register in which the music is to be performed. There are three kinds:

treble, or G clef, used for the upper stave of
keyboard music

𝄢	bass, or F clef, used for the lower stave of keyboard music
𝄡	C clef

INDICATIONS OF PITCH

♭	flat: lowering the note by a semi-tone
♯	sharp: raising the note by a semi-tone
♮	natural: returning a note to its original pitch

NOTE LENGTHS

Symbol	Name	Meaning	Rest
o	semibreve	whole note	▬
♩	minim	half note	▬
♩	crotchet	quarter note	𝄽
♪	quaver	eighth note	𝄾
♪	semi-quaver	sixteenth note	𝄿

TEMPO (the term used to denote variations in speed)

Term	Meaning
Accelerando	becoming faster
Ralendando, ritardando, ritenuto	becoming slower
Grave	very slow
Lento	slow
Largo	broadly
Adagio	in a leisurely manner
Andante	walking pace
Moderato	at a moderate speed
Allegro	lively, fairly fast
Vivace	fast
Presto	very fast
Prestissimo	as fast as possible

DYNAMICS (the term used to denote the volume of music)

Sign	Term	Meaning
pp	pianissimo	very soft
p	piano	soft
mp	mezzo-piano	moderately soft
mf	mezzo-forte	moderately loud
f	forte	loud
ff	fortissimo	very loud
<	crescendo	getting louder
>	diminuendo	getting softer

HALLMARKS

Hallmarks are the symbols stamped on gold, silver or platinum articles to indicate that they have been tested at an official Assay Office and that they conform to one of the legal standards. With certain exceptions, all gold, silver or platinum articles are required by law to be hallmarked before they are offered for sale.

Since 1 January 1999, UK hallmarks have consisted of three compulsory symbols: the sponsor's mark, the assay office mark, and the fineness (standard) mark. The date lettermark became voluntary on 1 January 1999. Additional marks have been authorized from time to time.

SPONSOR'S MARK

Instituted in England in 1363, the sponsor's mark was originally a device such as a bird or fleur-de-lis. Now it consists of the initial letters of the name or names of the manufacturer or firm. Where two or more sponsors have the same initials, there is a variation in the surrounding shield or style of letters.

FINENESS (STANDARD) MARK

The fineness (standard) mark indicates that the content of the precious metal in the alloy from which the article is made is not less than the legal standard. The legal standard is the minimum content of precious metal by weight in parts per thousand, and the standards are:

Gold	999	
	990	
	916.6	(22 carat)
	750	(18 carat)
	585	(14 carat)
	375	(9 carat)
Silver	999	
	958.4	(Britannia)
	925	(sterling)
	800	
Platinum	999	
	950	
	900	
	850	

The metals are marked as follows, if they are manufactured in the United Kingdom:

Gold – a crown followed by the millesimal figure for the standard, e.g. 916 for 22 carat (see table above)

Silver – Britannia silver: a full-length figure of Britannia. Sterling silver: a lion passant (England) or a lion rampant (Scotland)

   Britannia Silver

   Sterling Silver (England)

   Sterling Silver (Scotland)

Platinum – an orb

ASSAY OFFICE MARK

This mark identifies the particular assay office at which the article was tested and marked. The British assay offices are:

   London

   Birmingham

   Sheffield

   Edinburgh

Assay offices formerly existed in other towns, e.g. Chester, Exeter, Glasgow, Newcastle, Norwich and York, each having its own distinguishing mark.

DATE LETTER

The date letter shows the year in which an article was assayed and hallmarked. Each alphabetical cycle has a distinctive style of lettering or shape of shield. The date letters were different at the various assay offices and the particular office must be established from the assay office mark before reference is made to tables of date letters.

Since 1 January 1975, each office has used the same style of date letter and shield for all articles.

OTHER MARKS

FOREIGN GOODS

Foreign goods imported into the UK are required to be
hallmarked before sale, unless they already bear a convention
mark (*see* below) or a hallmark struck by an independent assay
office in the European Economic Area which is deemed to be
equivalent to a UK hallmark.

The following are the assay office marks for gold imported
articles. For silver and platinum the symbols remain the same but
the shields differ in shape.

 London

 Birmingham

 Sheffield

 Edinburgh

CONVENTION HALLMARKS

Special marks at authorized assay offices of the signatory
countries of the International Convention on Hallmarking
(Austria, the Czech Republic, Denmark, Finland, Ireland, the
Netherlands, Norway, Portugal, Sweden, Switzerland and the UK)
are legally recognized in the United Kingdom as approved
hallmarks. These consist of a sponsor's mark, a common control
mark, a fineness mark (arabic numerals showing the standard in
parts per thousand), and an assay office mark. There is no date
letter.

The fineness marks are:

Gold	750	(18 carat)
	585	(14 carat)
	375	(9 carat)
Silver	925	(sterling)
Platinum	950	

The common control marks are:

 Gold (18 carat)

 Silver

 Platinum

HERALDRY

TERMS

Achievement:	The complete pictorial display of arms comprising a shield, helmet, crest, torse, mantling and motto. Supporters, additional mottoes or rallying cries, decorations and insignia of office may also be depicted if the individual is entitled to them.
Blazon:	The formula describing the design of arms of a whole achievement; or, used as a verb, to make such a description.
Escutcheon:	A shield, especially a small shield placed on top of a larger to display particulary significant arms.

POINTS AND PARTS OF A SHIELD

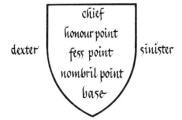

ORDINARIES

Ordinaries are simple geometric figures used in amory

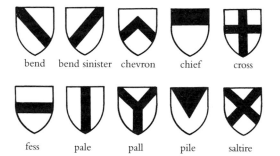

bend   bend sinister   chevron   chief   cross

fess   pale   pall   pile   saltire

DIVISIONS

parted per fess
= divided in
two horizontally

parted per pale
= divided in
two vertically

Impaling	dividing a shield vertically and placing arms in both halves
Quartering	dividing a shield in four and placing arms in all four quarters

TINCTURES

There are five colours, three stains and two metals

COLOURS

Gules	red
Azure	blue
Vert	green
Sable	black
Purpure	purple
Proper	an animal or object depicted in its natural colours

STAINS

Murrey	mulberry or maroon
Tenné	tawny orange
Sanguine	blood-coloured red

METALS

Or	gold; may be depicted as gilt, or painted as yellow or ochre
Argent	silver; may be painted as pale grey or be white

ANIMALS

rampant	rearing up with three paws outstretched
salient	springing up with both feet on the ground
passant	walking, usually with right forepaw raised
statant	standing, with all four feet down
sejant	sitting
couchant	lying, with head erect

Animals are usually facing to the dexter, but:

affronté	whole beast facing forward
gardant	face out to viewer
regardant	looking back over shoulder

BIRDS

close	wings folded in
rising	wings raised
displayed	fully frontal with both wings outstretched, tips up, talons stretched out on either side, tail spread and head turned to the dexter

Heads of birds are usually shown in profile, except for owls, which are always gardant.

LANGUAGE

PUNCTUATION MARKS AND ACCENTS

The list below gives the names of the punctuation marks and accents in common usage.

,	comma
;	semicolon
:	colon
.	full stop
?	question mark
!	exclamation mark
'	apostrophe
' '	single quotation marks
" "	double quotation marks
( )	parentheses
[ ]	square brackets
< >	angle brackets
{ }	curly brackets
-	hyphen
--	dash
{	brace
&	ampersand
★	asterisk
...	mark of omission/ellipsis
á	acute accent (a)
à	grave accent (a)
â	circumflex (a)
ç	cedilla (c)
ë	umlaut (diaresis) (e)
ñ	tilde (n)
š	caron (s)
å	ångström (a)

COLLECTIVE NOUNS FOR ANIMALS

The following terms for groups of animals are derived from medieval bestiaries.

Ants	army, column, state, swarm
Apes	shrewdness
Baboons	troop
Badger	cete, colony
Bears	sloth
Beavers	colony
Bees	cluster, erst, hive, swarm
Budgerigars	chatter
Camels	caravan, flock

Caterpillars	army
Cats	chowder, clowder, cluster
Chickens	brood, clutch, peep
Crows	clan, hover, murder
Dogs	cowardice, kennel, pack
Dolphins	pod, school
Doves	dole, flight, prettying
Eagles	convocation
Eels	swarm
Falcons	cast
Ferrets	business, cast, fesynes
Flamingos	flurry, regiment, skein
Flies	business, cloud, scraw, swarm
Foxes	earth, lead, skulk
Frogs	army, colony
Geese	gaggle
Giraffes	corps, herd, troop
Goldfinch	charm, chattering, chirp, drum
Goldfish	troubling
Grasshoppers	cloud
Greyhounds	brace, leash, pack
Grouse	brood, covey, pack
Hares	down, drove, husk, lie, trip
Hawks	cast
Hedgehogs	array
Heron	scattering, sedge, siege
Herring	army, gleam, shoal
Ibis	crowd
Jellyfish	brood, smuck
Lapwings	deceit, desert
Larks	exultation
Leopards	leap
Lions	flock, pride, sawt, souse, troop
Mackerel	school, shoal
Magpies	tiding, tittering
Mice	nest
Moles	company, labour, movement, mumble
Monkeys	troop
Mules	barren, cartload, pack, span
Nightingale	match, puddling, watch
Otters	bevy, family
Owls	parliament, stare
Partridges	covey
Peacocks	muster
Penguins	colony, rookery
Pheasants	brook, ostentation, pride, nye
Piglets	farrow
Pigs	litter, herd, sounder

Plover	congregation, flight, stand, wing
Quail	bevy, covey
Rabbits	bury, colony, nest, warren
Raccoons	nursery
Rats	colony
Ravens	unkindness
Rhinoceros	crash
Rooks	building, clamour, parliament
Sardines	family
Seals	harem, herd, pod, rookery
Snakes	den, pit
Snipe	walk, whisper, wish, wisp
Sparrows	host, surration, quarrel
Spiders	cluster, clutter
Squirrels	drey
Starlings	chattering, crowd, murmuration
Swans	bank, bevy, game, herd, squadron, teeme, wedge, whiteness
Thrush	mutation
Tigers	ambush
Toads	knab, knot
Trout	hover
Turkeys	dule, raffle, rafter
Turtle Doves	pitying
Turtles	bale, dole
Wasps	herd, nest, pladge
Whales	colony, gam, herd, pod, school
Woodcocks	covey, fall, flight, plump
Woodpeckers	descent

BOOKS OF THE BIBLE

The following list gives the commonly used abbreviations for the books of the Bible.

OLD TESTAMENT

Genesis	Gen.
Exodus	Exod.
Leviticus	Lev.
Numbers	Num.
Deuteronomy	Deut.
Joshua	Josh.
Judges	Judg.
Ruth	Ruth
1 Samuel	1 Sam.
2 Samuel	2 Sam.
1 Kings	1 Kgs.
2 Kings	2 Kgs.

1 Chronicles	1 Chr.
2 Chronicles	2 Chr.
Ezra	Ezra
Nehemiah	Neh.
Esther	Esther
Job	Job
Psalms	Ps.
Proverbs	Prov.
Ecclesiastes	Eccles.
Song of Solomon	S. of S.
Isaiah	Isa.
Jeremiah	Jer.
Lamentations	Lam.
Ezekiel	Ezek.
Daniel	Dan.
Hosea	Hos.
Joel	Joel
Amos	Amos
Obadiah	Obad.
Jonah	Jon.
Micah	Mic.
Nahum	Nah.
Habakkuk	Hab.
Zephaniah	Zeph.
Haggai	Hag.
Zechariah	Zech.
Malachi	Mal.

APOCRYPHA

1 Esdras	1 Esd.
2 Esdras	2 Esd.
Tobit	Tobit
Judith	Judith
Rest of Esther	Rest of Esth.
Wisdom of Solomon	Wisd.
Ecclesiasticus	Ecclus.
Baruch with the Epistle of Jeremy	Baruch and Ep. of Jer.
Song of the Three Holy Children	S. of III Ch.
History of Susanna	Sus.
Bel and the Dragon	Bel & Dr.
Prayer of Manasses	Pr. of Man.
1 Maccabees	1 Macc.
2 Maccabees	2 Macc.

NEW TESTAMENT

Matthew	Matt.
Mark	Mark
Luke	Luke
John	John
Acts	Acts
Romans	Rom.
1 Corinthians	1 Cor.
2 Corinthians	2 Cor.
Galatians	Gal.
Ephesians	Eph.
Philippians	Phil.
Colossians	Col.
1 Thessalonians	1 Thess.
2 Thessalonians	2 Thess.
1 Timothy	1 Tim.
2 Timothy	2 Tim.
Titus	Titus
Philemon	Philem.
Hebrews	Heb.
James	Jas.
1 Peter	1 Pet.
2 Peter	2 Pet.
1 John	1 John
2 John	2 John
3 John	3 John
Jude	Jude
Revelation	Rev.

BRITISH POLITICS

GENERAL ELECTIONS SINCE 1900

Year	Date	Party forming the Government
1900	28 Sept–24 Oct	Conservative
1906	12 Jan–7 Feb	Liberal
1910	14 Jan–9 Feb	Liberal
1910	2–19 Dec	Liberal
1918	14 Dec	Coalition*
1922	15 Nov	Conservative
1923	6 Dec	Coalition†
1924	29 Oct	Conservative
1929	30 May	Labour
1931	27 Oct	National Government‡
1935	14 Nov	Conservative
1945	5 July	Labour
1950	23 Feb	Labour
1951	25 Oct	Conservative
1955	26 May	Conservative
1959	8 Oct	Conservative
1964	15 Oct	Conservative
1966	31 March	Labour
1970	18 June	Conservative
1974	28 Feb	Labour
1974	10 Oct	Labour
1979	3 May	Conservative
1983	9 June	Conservative
1987	11 June	Conservative
1992	9 April	Conservative
1997	1 May	Labour

*Coalition of Coalition Unionist (335 seats), Coalition Liberal (133) and Coalition Labour (10); opposition parties 229 seats, including 28 Liberal and 63 Labour
†Coalition of Labour (191 seats) and Liberal (159); opposition parties 265 seats, including Conservative 258
‡National Government of Conservative (473 seats), Liberal National (35), Liberal (33) and National Labour (13); opposition parties 61 seats, including Labour 52 and Independent Liberal 4

PRIME MINISTERS

The accession of George I, who was unfamiliar with the English language, led to a disinclination on the part of the Sovereign to preside at meetings of his Ministers and caused the appearance of a Prime Minister, a position first acquired by Robert Walpole in 1721 and retained by him without interruption for 20 years and

326 days. The office of Prime Minister was officially recognized in 1905.

The Prime Minister, by tradition also First Lord of the Treasury and Minister for the Civil Service, is appointed by the Sovereign and is usually the leader of the party which enjoys, or can secure, a majority in the House of Commons. Other Ministers are appointed by the Sovereign on the recommendation of the Prime Minister, who also allocates functions amongst Ministers and has the power to obtain their resignation or dismissal individually.

Over the centuries there has been some variation in the determination of the dates of appointment of Prime Ministers. Where possible, the date given is that on which a new Prime Minister kissed the Sovereign's hands and accepted the commission to form a ministry. However, until the middle of the 19th century the dating of a commission or transfer of seals could be the date of taking office. Where the composition of the Government changed, e.g. became a coalition, but the Prime Minister remained the same, the date of the change of government is given.

Year appointed	
1721	Sir Robert Walpole, *Whig*
1742	The Earl of Wilmington, *Whig*
1743	Henry Pelham, *Whig*
1754	The Duke of Newcastle, *Whig*
1756	The Duke of Devonshire, *Whig*
1757	The Duke of Newcastle, *Whig*
1762	The Earl of Bute, *Tory*
1763	George Grenville, *Whig*
1765	The Marquess of Rockingham, *Whig*
1766	The Earl of Chatham, *Whig*
1767	The Duke of Grafton, *Whig*
1770	Lord North, *Tory*
1782 *March*	The Marquess of Rockingham, *Whig*
1782 *July*	The Earl of Shelburne, *Whig*
1783 *April*	The Duke of Portland, *Coalition*
1783 *Dec.*	William Pitt, *Tory*
1801	Henry Addington, *Tory*
1804	William Pitt, *Tory*
1806	The Lord Grenville, *Whig*
1807	The Duke of Portland, *Tory*
1809	Spencer Perceval, *Tory*
1812	The Earl of Liverpool, *Tory*
1827 *April*	George Canning, *Tory*
1827 *Aug.*	Viscount Goderich, *Tory*

Year appointed	
1828	The Duke of Wellington, *Tory*
1830	The Earl Grey, *Whig*
1834 *July*	The Viscount Melbourne, *Whig*
1834 *Nov.*	The Duke of Wellington, *Tory*
1834 *Dec.*	Sir Robert Peel, *Tory*
1835	The Viscount of Melbourne, *Whig*
1841	Sir Robert Peel, *Tory*
1846	Lord John Russell (later the Earl Russell), *Whig*
1852 *Feb.*	The Earl of Derby, *Tory*
1852 *Dec.*	The Earl of Aberdeen, *Peelite*
1855	The Viscount Palmerston, *Liberal*
1858	The Earl of Derby, *Conservative*
1859	The Viscount Palmerston, *Liberal*
1865	The Earl Russell, *Liberal*
1866	The Earl of Derby, *Conservative*
1868 *Feb.*	Benjamin Disraeli, *Conservative*
1868 *Dec.*	William Gladstone, *Liberal*
1874	Benjamin Disraeli, *Conservative*
1880	William Gladstone, *Liberal*
1885	The Marquess of Salisbury, *Conservative*
1886 *Feb.*	William Gladstone, *Liberal*
1886 *July*	The Marquess of Salisbury, *Conservative*
1892	William Gladstone, *Liberal*
1894	The Earl of Rosebery, *Liberal*
1895	The Marquess of Salisbury, *Conservative*
1902	Arthur Balfour, *Conservative*
1905	Sir Henry Campbell-Bannerman, *Liberal*
1908	Herbert Asquith, *Liberal*
1915	Herbert Asquith, *Coalition*
1916	David Lloyd-George, *Coalition*
1922	Andrew Bonar Law, *Conservative*
1923	Stanley Baldwin, *Conservative*
1924 *Jan.*	Ramsay MacDonald, *Labour*
1924 *Nov.*	Stanley Baldwin, *Conservative*
1929	Ramsay MacDonald, *Labour*
1931	Ramsay MacDonald, *Coalition*
1935	Stanley Baldwin, *Coalition*
1937	Neville Chamberlain, *Coalition*
1940	Winston Churchill, *Coalition*
1945 *May*	Winston Churchill, *Conservative*
1945 *July*	Clement Attlee, *Labour*
1951	Sir Winston Churchill, *Conservative*
1955	Sir Anthony Eden, *Conservative*
1957	Harold Macmillan, *Conservative*
1963	Sir Alec Douglas-Home, *Conservative*
1964	Harold Wilson, *Labour*
1970	Edward Heath, *Conservative*

1974	Harold Wilson, *Labour*
1976	James Callaghan, *Labour*
1979	Margaret Thatcher, *Conservative*
1990	John Major, *Conservative*
1997	Anthony Blair, *Labour*

LEADERS OF THE OPPOSITION

The office of Leader of the Opposition was officially recognized in 1937 and a salary was assigned to the post.

Year
appointed

1916	Herbert Asquith, *Liberal*
1918	William Adamson, *Labour*
1921	John Clynes, *Labour*
1922	Ramsay MacDonald, *Labour* (leader of official Opposition)
1924	Stanley Baldwin, *Conservative*
1929	Stanley Baldwin, *Conservative*
1931	Arthur Henderson, *Labour* (leader of Labour Opposition)
1931	George Lansbury, *Labour*
1935	Clement Attlee, *Labour*
1945	Clement Attlee, *Labour*
1945	Winston Churchill, *Conservative*
1951	Clement Attlee, *Labour*
1955	Hugh Gaitskell, *Labour*
1963	Harold Wilson, *Labour*
1965	Edward Heath, *Conservative*
1974	Edward Heath, *Conservative*
1970	Harold Wilson, *Labour*
1975	Margaret Thatcher, *Conservative*
1979	James Callaghan, *Labour*
1980	Michael Foot, *Labour*
1983	Neil Kinnock, *Labour*
1992	John Smith, *Labour*
1994	Anthony Blair, *Labour*
1997	William Hague, *Conservative*

SPEAKERS OF THE COMMONS SINCE 1660

The Speaker of the House of Commons is the spokesman and president of the Chamber. He or she is elected by the House at the beginning of each Parliament or when the previous Speaker retires or dies. The Speaker neither speaks in debates nor votes in divisions except when the voting is equal.

The appointment requires royal approbation before it is confirmed. The present Speaker is the 155th.

Parliament of England

Year
appointed

1660	Sir Harbottle Grimston
1661	Sir Edward Turner
1673	Sir Job Charlton
1678 *Feb.*	Sir Edward Seymour
1678 *April*	Sir Robert Sawyer
1679	Sir William Gregory
1680	Sir William Williams
1685	Sir John Trevor
1689	Henry Powle
1690	Sir John Trevor
1695	Paul Foley
1698	Sir Thomas Lyttleton
1701	Robert Harley *(Earl of Oxford and Mortimer)*
1705	John Smith

Parliament of Great Britain

1708	Sir Richard Onslow *(Lord Onslow)*
1710	William Bromley
1714	Sir Thomas Hanmer
1715	Spencer Compton *(Earl of Wilmington)*
1728	Arthur Onslow
1761	Sir John Cust
1770	Sir Fletcher Norton *(Lord Grantley)*
1780	Charles Cornwall
1789 *Jan.*	Hon. William Grenville *(Lord Grenville)*
1789 *June*	Henry Addington *(Viscount Sidmouth)*

Parliament of United Kingdom

1801	Sir John Mitford *(Lord Redesdale)*
1802	Charles Abbot *(Lord Colchester)*
1817	Charles Manners-Sutton *(Viscount Canterbury)*
1835	James Abercromby *(Lord Dunfermline)*
1839	Charles Shaw-Lefevre *(Viscount Eversley)*
1857	J. Evelyn Denison *(Viscount Ossington)*
1872	Sir Henry Brand *(Viscount Hampden)*
1884	Arthur Wellesley Peel *(Viscount Peel)*
1895	William Gully *(Viscount Selby)*
1905	James Lowther *(Viscount Ullswater)*
1921	John Whitley
1928	Hon. Edward Fitzroy
1943	Douglas Clifton-Brown *(Viscount Ruffside)*
1951	William Morrison *(Viscount Dunrossil)*
1959	Sir Harry Hylton-Foster

1965	Horace King *(Lord Maybray-King)*
1971	Selwyn Lloyd *(Lord Selwyn-Lloyd)*
1976	George Thomas *(Viscount Tonypandy)*
1983	Bernard Weatherill *(Lord Weatherill)*
1992	Betty Boothroyd

CHANCELLORS OF THE EXCHEQUER SINCE 1900

Year appointed	
1895	Sir Michael Hicks-Beach
1902	Charles Ritchie
1903	Austen Chamberlain
1905	Herbert Asquith
1908	David Lloyd George
1915	Reginald McKenna
1916	Andrew Bonar Law
1919	Austen Chamberlain
1921	Sir Robert Horne
1922	Stanley Baldwin
1923	Neville Chamberlain
1924 *Jan.*	Philip Snowden
1924 *Nov.*	Winston Churchill
1929	Philip Snowden
1931	Neville Chamberlain
1937	Sir John Simon
1940	Sir Kingsley Wood
1943	Sir John Anderson
1945	Hugh Dalton
1947	Sir Stafford Cripps
1950	Hugh Gaitskell
1951	R. A. Butler
1955	Harold Macmillan
1957	Peter Thorneycroft
1958	Derick Heathcoat Amory
1960	Selwyn Lloyd
1962	Reginald Maudling
1964	James Callaghan
1967	Roy Jenkins
1970 *June*	Iain Macleod
1970 *July*	Anthony Barber
1974	Denis Healey
1979	Sir Geoffrey Howe
1983	Nigel Lawson
1989	John Major
1990	Norman Lamont
1993	Kenneth Clarke
1997	Gordon Brown

SECRETARIES OF STATE FOR FOREIGN AFFAIRS SINCE 1900

In 1782 the Northern Department was converted into the Foreign Office, and Charles James Fox was appointed first Secretary of State for Foreign Affairs. With the merger of the Foreign Office and the Commonwealth Office on 1 October 1968 the post was redesignated as Secretary of State for Foreign and Commonwealth Affairs.

Year
appointed

1895	Marquess of Salisbury
1900	Marquess of Lansdowne
1905	Sir Edward Grey
1916	Arthur Balfour
1919	Earl Curzon
1924 *Jan.*	Ramsay MacDonald
1924 *Nov.*	Sir Austen Chamberlain
1929	Arthur Henderson
1931 *Aug.*	Marquess of Reading
1931 *Nov.*	Sir John Simon
1935 *June*	Sir Samuel Hoare
1935 *Dec.*	Anthony Eden
1938	Viscount Halifax
1940	Anthony Eden
1945	Ernest Bevin
1951 *March*	Herbert Morrison
1951 *Oct.*	Anthony Eden
1955 *April*	Harold Macmillan
1955 *Dec.*	Selwyn Lloyd
1960	Earl of Home
1963	R. A. Butler
1964	Patrick Gordon Walker
1965	Michael Stewart
1966	George Brown
1968	Michael Stewart
1970	Sir Alec Douglas-Home
1974	James Callaghan
1976	Anthony Crosland
1977	David Owen
1979	Lord Carrington
1982	Francis Pym
1983	Sir Geoffrey Howe
1989 *July*	John Major
1989 *Nov.*	Douglas Hurd
1995	Malcolm Rifkind
1997	Robin Cook

SECRETARIES OF STATE FOR THE HOME DEPARTMENT SINCE 1900

In 1782 the Southern Department was converted into the Home Office. The conduct of war was removed from the Home Secretary's hands in 1794 to a separate Secretary for War. Colonies were similarly transferred in 1801 to the Secretary for War and Colonies.

Year appointed	
1895	Sir Matthew White-Ridley
1900	Charles Ritchie
1902	Aretas Akers-Douglas
1905	Herbert Gladstone
1910	Winston Churchill
1911	Reginald McKenna
1915	Sir John Simon
1916 *Jan.*	Herbert Samuel
1916 *Dec.*	Sir George Cave
1919	Edward Shortt
1922	William Bridgeman
1924 *Jan.*	Arthur Henderson
1924 *Nov.*	Sir William Joynson-Hicks
1929	John Clynes
1931	Sir Herbert Samuel
1932	Sir John Gilmour
1935	Sir John Simon
1937	Sir Samuel Hoare
1939	Sir John Anderson
1940	Herbert Morrison
1945 *May*	Sir Donald Somervell
1945 *Aug.*	Chuter Ede
1951	Sir David Maxwell-Fyfe
1954	Gwilym Lloyd-George
1957	R. A. Butler
1962	Henry Brooke
1964	Sir Frank Soskice
1965	Roy Jenkins
1967	James Callaghan
1970	Reginald Maudling
1972	Robert Carr
1974	Roy Jenkins
1976	Merlyn Rees
1979	William Whitelaw
1983	Leon Brittan
1985	Douglas Hurd
1989	David Waddington

1990	Kenneth Baker
1992	Kenneth Clarke
1993	Michael Howard
1997	Jack Straw

LORD CHANCELLORS SINCE 1900

Year
appointed

1895	Lord Halsbury
1905	Lord Loreburn
1912	Lord Haldane
1915	Lord Buckmaster
1916	Lord Finlay
1919	Lord Birkenhead
1922	Viscount Cave
1924 *Jan.*	Viscount Haldane
1924 *Nov.*	Viscount Cave
1928	Lord Hailsham
1929	Lord Sankey
1935	Viscount Hailsham
1938	Lord Maugham
1939	Viscount Caldecote
1940	Viscount Simon
1945	Lord Jowitt
1951	Lord Simonds
1954	Viscount Kilmuir
1962	Lord Dilhorne
1964	Lord Gardiner
1970	Lord Hailsham of St Marylebone
1974	Lord Elwyn-Jones
1979	Lord Hailsham of St Marylebone
1987 *June*	Lord Havers
1987 *Oct.*	Lord Mackay of Clashfern
1997	Lord Irvine of Lairg

POLITICAL PARTIES

CONSERVATIVE PARTY

In the early 19th century the Tory Party became known as 'Conservative', to indicate that the preservation of national institutions was the leading principle of the party.

Until 1922, when the Conservatives were in opposition there were separate Leaders of the Conservative Party in the House of Commons and the House of Lords. In the following list, the leaders in the Commons for the relevant years are given (★).

LEADERS OF THE CONSERVATIVE PARTY

1900	Marquess of Salisbury
1902	Arthur Balfour
1911	Andrew Bonar Law★
1921	Austen Chamberlain★
1922	Andrew Bonar Law★
1923	Stanley Baldwin
1937	Neville Chamberlain
1940	Winston Churchill
1955	Sir Anthony Eden
1957	Harold Macmillan
1963	Sir Alec Douglas-Home
1965	Edward Heath
1975	Margaret Thatcher
1990	John Major
1997	William Hague

LABOUR PARTY

Labour candidates first stood for Parliament at the general election of 1892, when there were 27 standing as Labour or Liberal-Labour. In 1900 the Labour Representation Committee was set up in order to establish a distinct Labour group in Parliament. In 1906 the LRC became known as the Labour Party.

From 1922 to 1981, when in opposition, the Parliamentary Labour Party elected its Leader at the beginning of each session; most elections were uncontested.

CHAIRMEN OF THE PARLIAMENTARY LABOUR PARTY

1906	Keir Hardie
1908	Arthur Henderson
1910	George Barnes
1911	Ramsay MacDonald
1914	Arthur Henderson
1917	William Adamson

CHAIRMEN AND LEADERS OF THE PARLIAMENTARY LABOUR PARTY

1922	Ramsay MacDonald
1931	Arthur Henderson★
1932	George Lansbury
1935	Clement Attlee
1955	Hugh Gaitskell
1963	Harold Wilson

LEADERS OF THE PARLIAMENTARY LABOUR PARTY

1970	Harold Wilson
1976	James Callaghan

LEADERS OF THE LABOUR PARTY

1978	James Callaghan
1980	Michael Foot
1983	Neil Kinnock
1992	John Smith
1994	Anthony Blair

★Arthur Henderson lost his seat in the 1931 election. The acting leader of the Parliamentary Labour Party in 1931 was George Lansbury

LIBERAL PARTY

In 1828 the Whigs became known as 'Liberals', a name gradually accepted by the party to indicate its claim to be champions of political reform and progressive legislation.

The Liberal Party split in 1916 into two factions, which merged again following the 1922 election. In 1931 the party split into three factions: the Liberals, led by Sir Herbert Samuel; the Independent Liberals, led by David Lloyd George; and the National Liberals, led by Sir John Simon. The Independent Liberals rejoined the Liberals in the mid-1930s; the National Liberals gradually merged with the Conservative Party.

After 1981 the Liberal Party formed an alliance with the Social Democratic Party, and in 1988 a majority of the Liberals agreed on a merger with the SDP under the title Social and Liberal Democrats; since 1989 they have been known as the Liberal Democrats. A minority continue separately as the Liberal Party.

LEADERS OF THE LIBERAL PARTY

1900	Sir Henry Campbell-Bannerman
1908	Herbert Asquith
1926	David Lloyd George
1931	Sir Herbert Samuel
1935	Sir Archibald Sinclair

1945	Clement Davies
1956	Jo Grimond
1967	Jeremy Thorpe
1976	David Steel

LEADERS OF THE LIBERAL DEMOCRATS
1988	David Steel★
	Robert Maclennan★
1988	Paddy Ashdown
1999	Charles Kennedy

★David Steel and Robert Maclennan merged their respective parties into the Liberal Democrats and were joint leaders until a new leader was elected

SOCIAL DEMOCRATIC PARTY

The Council for Social Democracy was announced by four former Labour Cabinet Ministers in January 1981 and on 26 March 1981 the Social Democratic Party was launched. Later that year the SDP and the Liberal Party formed an electoral alliance. In 1988 a majority of the SDP agreed on a merger with the Liberal Party (see above) but a minority continued as a separate party under the SDP title. In 1990 it was decided to wind up the party organization and its three sitting MPs became independent social democrats.

LEADERS OF THE SDP
1982	Roy Jenkins
1983	David Owen
1987	Robert Maclennan
1988	David Owen

DEVOLUTION GOVERNMENT IN SCOTLAND AND WALES

THE SCOTTISH PARLIAMENT
Elected: 6 May 1999
First session: 12 May 1999
Official opening: 1 July 1999, at Edinburgh Assembly Hall
Number of Members: 129 (including the Presiding Officer)
First Minister, The Rt. Hon. Donald Dewar, MP, MSP (Lab.)
The Presiding Officer, The Rt. Hon. Sir David Steel, KBE

THE NATIONAL ASSEMBLY FOR WALES
Elected: 6 May 1999
First session: 10 May 1999
Official opening: 26 May 1999, at Crickhowell House, Cardiff
Number of Members: 60 (including the Presiding Officer)
First Secretary, The Rt. Hon. Alun Michael, MP, AM (Lab.)
The Presiding Officer, The Lord Elis-Thomas, AM

ROYALTY

THE BRITISH ROYAL FAMILY

THE SOVEREIGN

ELIZABETH II, by the Grace of God, of the United Kingdom of Great Britain and Northern Ireland and of her other Realms and Territories Queen, Head of the Commonwealth, Defender of the Faith
Born 21 April 1926
Ascended the throne 6 February 1952
Crowned 2 June 1953, at Westminster Abbey
Married 20 November 1947 HRH The Prince Philip, Duke of Edinburgh, KG, KT, OM, GBE, PC (*born* 10 June 1921)

CHILDREN OF THE QUEEN

HRH THE PRINCE OF WALES (Prince Charles), KG, KT, GCB, PC, *born* 14 November 1948
Married 1981 Lady Diana Spencer (Diana, Princess of Wales (1961–97)); marriage dissolved 1996
Children
(1) HRH Prince William of Wales, *born* 21 June 1982
(2) HRH Prince Henry of Wales, *born* 15 September 1984

HRH THE PRINCESS ROYAL (Princess Anne), KG, GCVO, *born* 15 August 1950
Married (1) 1973 Capt Mark Phillips, CVO; marriage dissolved 1992; (2) 1992 Capt Timothy Laurence, MVO, RN
Children
(1) Peter Phillips, *born* 15 November 1977
(2) Zara Phillips, *born* 15 May 1981

HRH THE DUKE OF YORK (Prince Andrew), CVO, *born* 19 February 1960
Married 1986 Sarah Ferguson (Sarah, Duchess of York); marriage dissolved 1996
Children
(1) HRH Princess Beatrice of York, *born* 8 August 1988
(2) HRH Princess Eugenie of York, *born* 23 March 1990

HRH THE EARL OF WESSEX (Prince Edward), CVO, *born* 10 March 1964
Married 1999 Sophie Rhys-Jones (HRH The Countess of Wessex)

SISTER OF THE QUEEN

HRH THE PRINCESS MARGARET, COUNTESS OF SNOWDON, CI, GCVO, *born* 21 August 1930, younger daughter

of King George VI and HM Queen Elizabeth the Queen Mother
Married 1960 Antony Armstrong-Jones (The Earl of Snowdon,
GCVO); marriage dissolved 1978
Children
(1) David, Viscount Linley, *born* 3 November 1961, *married* 1993
the Hon. Serena Stanhope and has a son, Hon. Charles Linley
(2) Lady Sarah Chatto, *born* 1 May 1964, *married* 1994 Daniel
Chatto, and has children: Samuel Chatto and Arthur Chatto

MOTHER OF THE QUEEN

HM QUEEN ELIZABETH THE QUEEN MOTHER, Lady of
the Garter, Lady of the Thistle, CI, GCVO, GBE, *born* 4 August
1900
Married 1923 (as Lady Elizabeth Bowes-Lyon) Prince Albert,
Duke of York, afterwards King George VI

AUNT OF THE QUEEN

HRH PRINCESS ALICE, DUCHESS OF GLOUCESTER,
GCB, CI, GCVO, GBE, *born* 25 December 1901
Married 1935 (as Lady Alice Montagu-Douglas-Scott) Prince
Henry, Duke of Gloucester, third son of King George V

COUSINS OF THE QUEEN

HRH THE DUKE OF GLOUCESTER (Prince Richard), KG,
GCVO, *born* 26 August 1944
Married 1972 Birgitte van Deurs (HRH The Duchess of
Gloucester, GCVO)
Children
(1) Alexander, Earl of Ulster, *born* 24 October 1974
(2) Lady Davina Windsor, *born* 19 November 1977
(3) Lady Rose Windsor, *born* 1 March 1980

HRH THE DUKE OF KENT (Prince Edward), KG, GCMG,
GCVO, *born* 9 October 1935
Married 1961 Katharine Worsley (HRH The Duchess of Kent,
GCVO)
Children
(1) George, Earl of St Andrews, *born* 26 June 1962, *married* 1988
Sylvana Tomaselli, and has children: Edward, Lord Downpatrick,
Lady Marina Charlotte Windsor and Lady Amelia Windsor
(2) Lady Helen Taylor, *born* 28 April 1964, *married* 1992 Timothy
Taylor, and has children: Columbus Taylor and Cassius Taylor
(3) Lord Nicholas Windsor, *born* 25 July 1970

HRH PRINCESS ALEXANDRA, THE HON. LADY
OGILVY, GCVO, *born* 25 December 1936
Married 1963 The Rt. Hon. Sir Angus Ogilvy, KCVO

Children
(1) James Ogilvy, *born* 29 February 1964, *married* 1988 Julia Rawlinson, and has children: Flora Ogilvy and Alexander Ogilvy
(2) Marina, Mrs Mowatt, *born* 31 July 1966, *married* 1990 Paul Mowatt (marriage dissolved 1997), and has children: Zenouska Mowatt and Christian Mowatt

HRH PRINCE MICHAEL OF KENT, KCVO, *born* 4 July 1942
Married 1978 Baroness Marie-Christine von Reibnitz (HRH Princess Michael of Kent)
Children
(1) Lord Frederick Windsor, *born* 6 April 1979
(2) Lady Gabriella Windsor, *born* 23 April 1981

ORDER OF SUCCESSION TO THE THRONE

1	HRH The Prince of Wales
2	HRH Prince William of Wales
3	HRH Prince Henry of Wales
4	HRH The Duke of York
5	HRH Princess Beatrice of York
6	HRH Princess Eugenie of York
7	HRH The Earl of Wessex
8	HRH The Princess Royal
9	Peter Phillips
10	Zara Phillips
11	HRH The Princess Margaret, Countess of Snowdon
12	Viscount Linley
13	Hon. Charles Linley
14	Lady Sarah Chatto
15	Samuel Chatto
16	Arthur Chatto
17	HRH The Duke of Gloucester
18	Earl of Ulster
19	Lady Davina Windsor
20	Lady Rose Windsor
21	HRH The Duke of Kent
22	Baron Downpatrick
23	Lady Marina Charlotte Windsor
24	Lady Amelia Windsor
25	Lord Nicholas Windsor
26	Lady Helen Taylor
27	Columbus Taylor
28	Cassius Taylor
29	Lord Frederick Windsor
30	Lady Gabriella Windsor
31	HRH Princess Alexandra, the Hon. Lady Ogilvy
32	James Ogilvy

33   Alexander Ogilvy
34   Flora Ogilvy
35   Marina, Mrs Paul Mowatt
36   Christian Mowatt
37   Zenouska Mowatt
38   The Earl of Harewood

The Earl of St Andrews and HRH Prince Michael of Kent lost their right of succession to the throne through marriage to a Roman Catholic. Their children remain in succession provided that they are in communion with the Church of England

KINGS AND QUEENS

ENGLISH KINGS AND QUEENS, 927 TO 1603

HOUSES OF CERDIC AND DENMARK

Reign

927–39	Æthelstan (?–939)
939–46	Edmund I (921–46)
946–55	Eadred (?–955)
959–75	Edgar I (943–75)
975–78	Edward I (the Martyr) (*c.*962–978)
978–1016	Æthelred (the Unready) (*c.*968/969–1016)
1016	Edmund II (Ironside) (before 993–1016)
1016–35	Cnut (Canute) (*c.*995–1035)
1035–40	Harold I (Harefoot) (*c.*1016/17–1040)
1040–42	Harthacnut (*c.*1018–1042)
1042–66	Edward II (the Confessor) (*c.*1002/5–1066)
1066	Harold II (Godwinesson) (*c.*1020–1066)

THE HOUSE OF NORMANDY

1066–87	William I (the Conqueror) (*c.*1027–1087)
1087–1100	William II (Rufus) (*c.*1056/60–1100)
1100–35	Henry I (Beauclerk) (1068–1135)
1135–54	Stephen (before 1100–1154)

THE HOUSE OF ANJOU (PLANTAGANETS)

1154–89	Henry II (Curtmantle) (1133–89)
1189–99	Richard I (Coeur de Lion) (1157–99)
1199–1216	John (Lackland) (1167–1216)
1216–72	Henry III (1207–72)
1272–1307	Edward I (Longshanks) (1239–1307)
1307–27	Edward II (1284–1327)
1327–77	Edward III (1312–77)
1377–99	Richard II (1367–1400)

THE HOUSE OF LANCASTER

1399–1413	Henry IV (1366–1413)
1413–22	Henry V (1387–1422)
1422–71	Henry VI (1421–71)

THE HOUSE OF YORK

1461–83	Edward IV (1442–83)
1483	Edward V (1470–83)
1483–85	Richard III (1452–85)

THE HOUSE OF TUDOR

1485–1509	Henry VII (1457–1509)
1509–47	Henry VIII (1491–1547)
1547–53	Edward VI (1537–53)
1553	Jane (1537–54)
1553–58	Mary I (1516–58)
1558–1603	Elizabeth I (1533–1603)

BRITISH KINGS AND QUEENS SINCE 1603

THE HOUSE OF STUART

Reign

1603–25	James I (VI of Scotland) (1566–1625)
1625–49	Charles I (1600–49)
	Commonwealth declared 19 May 1649
1649–53	Government by a council of state
1653–58	Oliver Cromwell, Lord Protector
1658–59	Richard Cromwell, Lord Protector
	Restoration of the monarchy
1660–85	Charles II (1630–85)
1685–88	James II (VII of Scotland) (1633–1701)
	Interregnum 11 December 1688 to 12 February 1689
1689–1702	William III (1650–1702)
1689–94	Mary II (1662–94)
1702–14	Anne (1665–1714)

THE HOUSE OF HANOVER

1714–27	George I (Elector of Hanover) (1660–1727)
1727–60	George II (1683–1760)
1760–1820	George III (1738–1820)
	Regency 1811–20
	Prince of Wales regent owing to the insanity of George III
1820–30	George IV (1762–1830)
1830–37	William IV (1765–1837)
1837–1901	Victoria (1819–1901)

THE HOUSE OF SAXE-COBURG AND GOTHA

1901–10   Edward VII (1841–1910)

THE HOUSE OF WINDSOR

1910–36   George V (1865–1936)
1936   Edward VIII (1894–1972)
1936–52   George VI (1895–1952)
1952–   Elizabeth II (1926–)

KINGS AND QUEENS OF SCOTS, 1016 TO 1603

Reign
1016–34   Malcolm II (*c*.954–1034)

THE HOUSE OF ATHOLL

1034–40   Duncan I
1040–57   Macbeth (*c*.1005–1057)
1057–58   Lulach (*c*.1032–1058)
1058–93   Malcolm III (Canmore) (*c*.1031–1093)
1093–97   Donald III Ban (*c*.1033–1100)
             Deposed May 1094, restored November 1094
1094   Duncan II (*c*.1060–1094)
1097–1107   Edgar (*c*.1074–1107)
1107–24   Alexander I (The Fierce) (*c*.1077–1124)
1124–53   David I (The Saint) (*c*.1085–1153)
1153–65   Malcolm IV (The Maiden) (*c*.1141–1165)
1165–1214   William I (The Lion) (*c*.1142–1214)
1214–49   Alexander II (1198–1249)
1249–86   Alexander III (1241–86)
1286–90   Margaret (The Maid of Norway) (1283–90)
             First Interregnum 1290–92
             Throne disputed by 13 competitors. Crown
             awarded to John Balliol by adjudication of Edward
                 I of England

THE HOUSE OF BALLIOL

1292–96   John (Balliol) (*c*.1250–1313)
             Second Interregnum 1296–1306
             Edward I of England declared John Balliol to have
             forfeited the throne for contumacy in 1296 and
             took the government of Scotland into his own
             hands

THE HOUSE OF BRUCE

1306–29   Robert I (Bruce) (1274–1329)
1329–71   David II (1324–71)
             1332 Edward Balliol, son of John Balliol, crowned
             King of Scots September, expelled December
1333–36   Edward Balliol restored as King of Scots

THE HOUSE OF STEWART

1371–90	Robert II (Stewart) (1316–90)
1390–1406	Robert III (c.1337–1406)
1406–37	James I (1394–1437)
1437–60	James II (1430–60)
1460–88	James III (1452–88)
1488–1513	James IV (1473–1513)
1513–42	James V (1512–42)
1542–67	Mary (1542–87)
1567–1625	James VI (and I of England) (1566–1625)
	Succeeded 1603 to the English throne, so joining the English and Scottish crowns

WELSH SOVEREIGNS AND PRINCES

Wales was ruled by sovereign princes from the earliest times until the death of Llywelyn in 1282. The first English Prince of Wales was the son of Edward I, who was born in Caernarvon town on 25 April 1284. According to a discredited legend, he was presented to the Welsh chieftains as their prince, in fulfilment of a promise that they should have a prince who 'could not speak a word of English' and should be native born. This son, who afterwards became Edward II, was created 'Prince of Wales and Earl of Chester' at the Lincoln Parliament on 7 February 1301.

The title Prince of Wales is borne after individual conferment and is not inherited at birth, though some Princes have been declared and styled Prince of Wales but never formally so created (s.). The title was conferred on Prince Charles by The Queen on 26 July 1958. He was invested at Caernarvon on 1 July 1969.

INDEPENDENT PRINCES, 844 TO 1282

844–78	Rhodri the Great
878–916	Anarawd, son of Rhodri
916–50	Hywel Dda, the Good
950–79	Iago ab Idwal (or Ieuaf)
979–85	Hywel ab Ieuaf, the Bad
985–86	Cadwallon, his brother
986–99	Maredudd ab Owain ap Hywel Dda
999–1008	Cynan ap Hywel ab Ieuaf
1018–23	Llywelyn ap Seisyll
1023–39	Iago ab Idwal ap Meurig
1039–63	Gruffydd ap Llywelyn ap Seisyll
1063–75	Bleddyn ap Cynfyn
1075–81	Trahaern ap Caradog
1081–1137	Gruffydd ap Cynan ab Iago
1137–70	Owain Gwynedd
1170–94	Dafydd ab Owain Gwynedd

1194–1240	Llywelyn Fawr, the Great
1240–46	Dafydd ap Llywelyn
1246–82	Llywelyn ap Gruffydd ap Llywelyn

ENGLISH PRINCES SINCE 1301

1301	Edward (Edward II)
1343	Edward the Black Prince, son of Edward III
1376	Richard (Richard II), son of the Black Prince
1399	Henry of Monmouth (Henry V)
1454	Edward of Westminster, son of Henry VI
1471	Edward of Westminster (Edward V)
1483	Edward, son of Richard III (d. 1484)
1489	Arthur Tudor, son of Henry VII
1504	Henry Tudor (Henry VIII)
1610	Henry Stuart, son of James I (d. 1612)
1616	Charles Stuart (Charles I)
c.1638 (s.)	Charles Stuart (Charles II)
1688 (s.)	James Francis Edward Stuart (The Old Pretender), son of James II
1714	George Augustus (George II)
1729	Frederick Lewis, son of George II (d. 1751)
1751	George William Frederick (George III)
1762	George Augustus Frederick (George IV)
1841	Albert Edward (Edward VII)
1901	George (George V)
1910	Edward (Edward VIII)
1958	Charles, son of Elizabeth II

PRINCESSES ROYAL

The style Princess Royal is conferred at the Sovereign's discretion on his or her eldest daughter. It is an honorary title, held for life, and cannot be inherited or passed on. It was first conferred on Princess Mary, daughter of Charles I, in approximately 1642.

c.1642	Princess Mary (1631–60), daughter of Charles I
1727	Princess Anne (1709–59), daughter of George II
1766	Princess Charlotte (1766–1828), daughter of George III
1840	Princess Victoria (1840–1901), daughter of Victoria
1905	Princess Louise (1867–1931), daughter of Edward VII
1932	Princess Mary (1897–1965), daughter of George V
1987	Princess Anne (b. 1950), daughter of Elizabeth II

WORLD MONARCHIES

The following is a list of those countries of the world that are
monarchies or principalities, showing the head of state and
his/her date of accession to the throne.

Bahrain	Shaikh Hamad bin Isa al-Khalifa, acceded 7 March 1999
Belgium	King Albert II, acceded 9 August 1993
Bhutan	King Jigme Singye Wangchuk, acceded July 1972
Brunei	Sultan Hassanal Bolkiah, acceded 1967
Cambodia	King Sihanouk, acceded 24 September 1993
Denmark	Queen Margrethe II, acceded 14 January 1972
Japan	Emperor Akihito, acceded 8 January 1989
Jordan	King Abdullah bin Hussein, acceded 7 February 1999
Kuwait	Shaikh Jabir al-Ahmad al-Jabir al-Sabah, acceded 31 December 1977
Lesotho	King Letsie III, acceded February 1996
Liechtenstein	Prince Hans Adam II, acceded 13 November 1989
Luxembourg	Grand Duke Jean, acceded 12 November 1964
Malaysia	Yang di-Pertuan Agong Salehuddin Abdul Aziz, elected head of state February 1999
Monaco	Prince Rainier III, acceded 9 May 1949
Morocco	King Mohammed VI, acceded 23 July 1999
Nepal	King Birendra Bir Bikram Shah Dev, acceded 31 January 1972
The Netherlands	Queen Beatrix, acceded 30 April 1980
Norway	King Harald V, acceded 17 January 1991
Oman	Sultan Qaboos bin Said, acceded 23 July 1970
Qatar	Shaikh Hamad bin Khalifa al-Thani, acceded 27 June 1995
Samoa	Susuga Malietoa Tanumafili II, acceded 15 April 1963
Saudi Arabia	King Fahd, acceded 1 June 1982
Spain	King Juan Carlos I, acceded 22 November 1975
Swaziland	King Mswati III, acceded 25 April 1986
Sweden	King Carl XVI Gustaf, acceded 15 September 1973
Thailand	King Bhumibol Adulyadej, acceded 9 June 1946
Tonga	King Taufa'ahau Tupou IV, acceded 16 December 1965

United Arab Emirates	Sheikh Zayed bin Sultan al-Nahyan, acceded 1971
United Kingdom	Queen Elizabeth II★, acceded 6 February 1952

★ Also head of state in Antigua and Barbuda, Australia, The Bahamas, Barbados, Belize, Canada, Grenada, Jamaica, New Zealand, Papua New Guinea, St Christopher and Nevis, St Lucia, St Vincent and the Grenadines, Solomon Islands and Tuvalu

PEOPLE

PRESIDENTS OF THE USA

Year
inaugurated

1789	George Washington (1732–99), *Federation*
1797	John Adams (1735–1826), *Federation*
1801	Thomas Jefferson (1743–1826), *Republican*
1809	James Madison (1751–1836), *Republican*
1817	James Monroe (1758–1831), *Republican*
1825	John Quincy Adams (1767–1848), *Republican*
1829	Andrew Jackson (1767–1845), *Democrat*
1837	Martin Van Buren (1782–1862), *Democrat*
1841	William Harrison (1773–1841) (died in office), *Whig*
1841	John Tyler (1790–1862) (elected as Vice-President), *Whig*
1845	James Polk (1795–1849), *Democrat*
1849	Zachary Taylor (1784–1850) (died in office), *Whig*
1850	Millard Fillmore (1800–1874) (elected as Vice-President), *Whig*
1853	Franklin Pierce (1804–69), *Democrat*
1857	James Buchanan (1791–1868), *Democrat*
1861	Abraham Lincoln (1809–65) (assassinated in office), *Republican*
1865	Andrew Johnson (1808–75) (elected as Vice-President), *Republican*
1869	Ulysses Grant (1822–85), *Republican*
1877	Rutherford Hayes (1822–93), *Republican*
1881	James Garfield (1831–81) (assassinated in office), *Republican*
1881	Chester Arthur (1830–86) (elected as Vice-President), *Republican*
1885	Grover Cleveland (1837–1908), *Democrat*
1889	Benjamin Harrison (1833–1901), *Republican*
1893	Grover Cleveland (1837–1908), *Democrat*
1897	William McKinley (1843–1901) (assassinated in office), *Republican*
1901	Theodore Roosevelt (1858–1919) (elected as Vice-President), *Republican*
1909	William Taft (1857–1930), *Republican*
1913	Woodrow Wilson (1856–1924), *Democrat*
1921	Warren Harding (1865–1923) (died in office), *Republican*
1923	Calvin Coolidge (1872–1933) (elected as Vice-President), *Republican*
1929	Herbert Hoover (1874–1964), *Republican*

1933*	Franklin Roosevelt (1882–1945) (died in office), *Democrat*
1945	Harry Truman (1884–1972) (elected as Vice-President), *Democrat*
1953	Dwight Eisenhower (1890–1969), *Republican*
1961	John Kennedy (1917–63) (assassinated in office), *Democrat*
1963	Lyndon Johnson (1908–73) (elected as Vice-President), *Democrat*
1969	Richard Nixon (1913–94), *Republican*
1974†	Gerald Ford (1913–), *Republican*
1977	James Carter (1924–), *Democrat*
1981	Ronald Reagan (1911–), *Republican*
1989	George Bush (1924–), *Republican*
1993	William Clinton (1946–), *Democrat*

* Re-elected 5 November 1940, the first case of a third term; re-elected for a fourth term 7 November 1944
†Appointed under the provisions of the 25th Amendment

SECRETARIES-GENERAL OF THE UNITED NATIONS

1946 – 53	Trygve Lie (Norway)
1953 – 61	Dag Hammarskjöld (Sweden)
1961 – 71	U. Thant (Burma)
1971 – 81	Kurt Waldheim (Austria)
1981 – 91	Javier Pérez de Cuéllar (Peru)
1991 – 6	Boutros Boutros-Ghali (Egypt)
1996 –	Kofi Annan (Ghana)

ARCHBISHOPS OF CANTERBURY
SINCE THE ENGLISH REFORMATION

Year appointed

1533	Thomas Cranmer
1556	Reginald Pole
1559	Matthew Parker
1576	Edmund Grindal
1583	John Whitgift
1604	Richard Bancroft
1611	George Abbot
1633	William Laud
1660	William Juxon
1663	Gilbert Sheldon

Year
appointed

1678	William Sancroft
1691	John Tillotson
1695	Thomas Tenison
1716	William Wake
1737	John Potter
1747	Thomas Herring
1757	Matthew Hutton
1758	Thomas Secker
1768	Frederick Cornwallis
1783	John Moore
1805	Charles Manners-Sutton
1828	William Howley
1848	John Bird Sumner
1862	Charles Longley
1868	Archibald Campbell Tait
1883	Edward White Benson
1896	Frederick Temple
1903	Randall Davidson
1928	Cosmo Lang
1942	William Temple
1945	Geoffrey Fisher
1961	Michael Ramsey
1974	Donald Coggan
1980	Robert Runcie
1991	George Carey

ARCHBISHOPS OF YORK
SINCE THE ENGLISH REFORMATION

Year
appointed

1531	Edward Lee
1545	Robert Holgate
1555	Nicholas Heath
1561	Thomas Young
1570	Edmund Grindal
1577	Edwin Sandys
1589	John Piers
1595	Matthew Hutton
1606	Tobias Matthew
1628	George Montaigne
1629	Samuel Harsnett
1632	Richard Neile
1641	John Williams
1660	Accepted Frewen
1664	Richard Sterne

1683	John Dolben
1688	Thomas Lamplugh
1691	John Sharp
1714	William Dawes
1724	Launcelot Blackburn
1743	Thomas Herring
1747	Matthew Hutton
1757	John Gilbert
1761	Robert Hay Drummond
1777	William Markham
1808	Edward Vernon Harcourt
1847	Thomas Musgrave
1860	Charles Longley
1862	William Thomson
1891	William Connor Magee
1891	William Maclagan
1909	Cosmo Lang
1929	William Temple
1942	Cyril Garbett
1956	Michael Ramsey
1961	Donald Coggan
1975	Stuart Blanch
1983	John Habgood
1995	David Hope

POPES

SINCE THE ENGLISH REFORMATION

Year
elected

1523	Clement VII
1534	Paul III
1550	Julius III
1555	Marcellus II
1555	Paul IV
1559	Pius IV
1566	St Pius V
1572	Gregory XIII
1585	Sixtus V
1590	Urban VII
1590	Gregory XIV
1591	Innocent IX
1592	Clement VIII
1605	Leo XI
1605	Paul V
1621	Gregory XV
1623	Urban VIII
1644	Innocent X

Year elected	
1655	Alexander VII
1667	Clement IX
1670	Clement X
1676	Innocent XI
1689	Alexander VIII
1691	Innocent XII
1700	Clement XI
1721	Innocent XIII
1724	Benedict XIII
1730	Clement XII
1740	Benedict XIV
1758	Clement XIII
1769	Clement XIV
1775	Pius VI
1800	Pius VII
1823	Leo XII
1829	Pius VIII
1831	Gregory XVI
1846	Pius IX
1878	Leo XIII
1903	Pius X
1914	Benedict XV
1922	Pius XI
1939	Pius XII
1958	John XXIII
1963	Paul VI
1978	John Paul I
1978	John Paul II

PRESIDENTS OF THE ROYAL ACADEMY

The President is elected by members of the Royal Academy from among their number and is subject only to the authority of the Sovereign. The post was usually held for life until the early 20th century. The President now retires at his own discretion.

Year appointed	
1768	Sir Joshua Reynolds (1723–92)
1792	Benjamin West (1738–1820)
1805	James Wyatt (1746–1813)
1806	Benjamin West (1738–1820)
1820	Sir Thomas Lawrence (1769–1830)
1830	Sir Martin Shee (1770–1850)
1850	Sir Charles Eastlake (1793–1865)
1866	Sir Francis Grant (1803–78)
1878	Lord Leighton (1830–96)

1896	Sir John Millais (1829–96)
1896	Sir Edward Poynter (1836–1919)
1919	Sir Aston Webb (1849–1930)
1924	Sir Francis Dicksee (1853–1928)
1928	Sir William Llewellyn (1863–1941)
1938	Sir Edwin Lutyens (1869–1944)
1944	Sir Alfred Munnings (1878–1959)
1949	Sir Gerald Kelly (1879–1972)
1954	Sir Albert Richardson (1880–1964)
1956	Sir Charles Wheeler (1892–1974)
1966	Sir Thomas Monnington (1902–76)
1976	Sir Hugh Casson (1910–)
1984	Sir Roger de Grey (1918–95)
1993	Sir Philip Dowson* (1924–)

*Retires December 1999

PRESIDENTS OF THE ROYAL SOCIETY

The Royal Society received a charter from Charles II on 22 April 1662, when it was incorporated as a body politic and corporate under the appellation of The President, Council and Fellowship of the Royal Society of London, for improving Natural Knowledge.

*Year
appointed*

1662	Viscount Brouncker (?1620–84)
1677	Sir Joseph Williamson (1633–1701)
1680	Sir Christopher Wren (1632–1723)
1682	Sir John Hoskins, Bt. (1634–1705)
1683	Sir Cyril Wyche (?1632–1707)
1684	Samuel Pepys (1633–1703)
1686	Earl of Carbery (1640–1712/13)
1689	Earl of Pembroke (1656–1732/3)
1690	Sir Robert Southwell (1635–1702)
1695	Earl of Halifax (1661–1715)
1698	Lord Somers (1652–1716)
1703	Sir Isaac Newton (1642–1727)
1727	Sir Hans Sloane, Bt. (1660–1753)
1741	Martin Folkes (1690–1754)
1752	Earl of Macclesfield (1697–1764)
1764	Earl of Morton (1702–68)
1768	Sir James Burrow (1701–82)
1768	James West (?1704–72)
1772	Sir John Pringle, Bt. (1707–82)
1778	Sir Joseph Banks, Bt. (1743–1820)
1820	William Hyde Wollaston (1766–1828)
1820	Sir Humphrey Davy, Bt. (1778–1829)

Year
appointed

1827	Davies Gilbert (1767–1839)
1830	Duke of Sussex (1773–1843)
1838	Marquess of Northampton (1790–1851)
1848	Earl of Rosse (1800–1867)
1854	Lord Wrottesley (1798–1867)
1858	Sir Benjamin Brodie, Bt. (1783–1862)
1861	Sir Edward Sabine (1788–1883)
1871	Sir George Biddell Airy (1801–92)
1873	Sir Joseph Dalton Hooker (1817–1911)
1878	William Spottiswoode (1825–83)
1883	Thomas Henry Huxley (1825–95)
1885	Sir George Stokes, Bt. (1819–1903)
1890	Lord Kelvin (1824–1907)
1895	Lord Lister (1827–1912)
1900	Sir William Huggins (1824–1910)
1905	Lord Rayleigh (1842–1919)
1908	Sir Archibald Geikie (1835–1924)
1913	Sir William Crookes (1832–1919)
1915	Sir Joseph John Thomson (1856–1940)
1920	Sir Charles Scott Sherrington (1857–1952)
1925	Lord Rutherford (1871–1937)
1930	Sir Frederick Gowland Hopkins (1861–1947)
1935	Sir William Henry Bragg (1862–1942)
1940	Sir Henry Dale (1875–1968)
1945	Sir Robert Robinson (1886–1975)
1950	Lord Adrian (1889–1977)
1955	Sir Cyril Hinshelwood (1897–1967)
1960	Lord Florey (1898–1968)
1965	Lord Blackett (1897–1974)
1970	Sir Alan Hodgkin (1914–)
1975	Lord Todd (1907–97)
1980	Sir Andrew Huxley (1917–)
1985	Lord Porter of Luddenham (1920–)
1990	Sir Michael Atiyah (1929–)
1996	Sir Aaron Klug (1926–)

ASTRONOMERS ROYAL

Instituted in 1675, the title of Astronomer Royal was given to the director of the Royal Greenwich Observatory until 1975. Currently it is an honorary title for an outstanding astronomer, who receives a stipend of approximately £100 a year.

Year
appointed

1675	John Flamsteed (1646–1719)

1720	Edmund Halley (1656–1742)
1742	James Bradley (1693–1762)
1762	Nathaniel Bliss (1700–64)
1765	Nevil Maskelyne (1732–1811)
1811	John Pond (1767–1836)
1835	Sir George Airy (1801–92)
1881	Sir William Christie (1845–1922)
1910	Sir Frank Dyson (1868–1939)
1933	Sir Harold Jones (1890–1960)
1955	Sir Richard Woolley (1906–86)
1972	Sir Martin Ryle (1918–84)
1982	Sir Francis Graham-Smith (1923–)
1991	Sir Arnold Wolfendale (1927–)
1995	Sir Martin Rees (1942–)

MASTERS OF THE QUEEN'S (KING'S) MUSIC

'Master of the King's Music' was the title given to the official who presided over the court band during the reign of Charles I. The first Master was appointed in 1626. Today the Master is expected to organize the music for state occasions and to write new music for them, although there are no fixed duties. The post is held for life and the Master receives an annual honorarium of approximately £100.

Year
appointed

1626	Nicholas Lanier (1588–1666)
1666	Louis Grabu (?–1674)
1674	Nicholas Staggins (1650–1700)
1700	John Eccles (1668–1735)
1735	Maurice Greene (1695–1755)
1755	William Boyce (1710–79)
1779	John Stanley (1713–86)
1786	Sir William Parsons (1746–1817)
1817	William Shield (1748–1829)
1829	Christian Kramer (?–1834)
1834	François (Franz) Cramer (1772–1848)
1848	George Anderson (?–1870)
1870	Sir William Cusins (1833–93)
1893	Sir Walter Parratt (1841–1924)
1924	Sir Edward Elgar (1857–1934)
1934	Sir Henry Walford Davies (1869–1941)
1941	Sir Arnold Bax (1883–1953)
1953	Sir Arthur Bliss (1891–1975)
1975	Malcolm Williamson (1931–)

POETS LAUREATE

This title is conferred by letters patent on the post attached to the royal household. The post was officially established in 1670 when John Dryden became Poet Laureate, although Ben Jonson was considered to have been the first 'official' laureate. It is customary for the Poet Laureate to write verse to mark events of national importance. The Poet Laureate currently receives an honorarium of approximately £100 a year. The post is held for life.

Year appointed	
1616	Ben Jonson (1572–1637)
1638	Sir William D'Avenant (1606–68)

Year appointed	
1670	John Dryden (1631–89)
1689	Thomas Shadwell (1642–92)
1692	Nahum Tate (1652–1715)
1715	Nicholas Rowe (1674–1718)
1718	Laurence Eusden (1688–1730)
1730	Colley Cibber (1671–1757)
1757	William Whitehead (1715–85)
1785	Thomas Warton (1728–90)
1790	Henry Pye (1745–1813)
1813	Robert Southey (1774–1843)
1843	William Wordsworth (1770–1850)
1850	Alfred, Lord Tennyson (1809–92)
1896	Alfred Austin (1835–1913)
1913	Robert Bridges (1844–1930)
1930	John Masefield (1878–1967)
1968	Cecil Day Lewis (1904–72)
1972	Sir John Betjeman (1906–84)
1984	Ted Hughes (1930–98)
1999	Andrew Motion (1952–)

ETIQUETTE

FORMS OF ADDRESS

This list covers the forms of address for peers, baronets and knights, their wife and children, and Privy Counsellors.

Both formal and social forms of address are given where usage differs; nowadays, the social form is generally preferred to the formal, which increasingly is used only for official documents and on very formal occasions.

F— represents forename
S— represents surname

BARON
Envelope (formal), The Right Hon. Lord—; (social), The Lord—.
Letter (formal), My Lord; (social), Dear Lord—.
Spoken, Lord—.

BARON'S WIFE
Envelope (formal), The Right Hon. Lady—; (social), The Lady—.
Letter (formal), My Lady; (social), Dear Lady—.
Spoken, Lady—.

BARON'S CHILDREN
Envelope, The Hon. F— S—.
Letter, Dear Mr/Miss/Mrs S—.
Spoken, Mr/Miss/Mrs S—.

BARONESS IN OWN RIGHT
Envelope, may be addressed in same way as a Baron's wife or, if she prefers (formal), The Right Hon. the Baroness—; (social), The Baroness—.
Otherwise as for a Baron's wife.

BARONET
Envelope, Sir F— S—, Bt.
Letter (formal), Dear Sir; (social), Dear Sir F—.
Spoken, Sir F—.

BARONET'S WIFE
Envelope, Lady S—.
Letter (formal), Dear Madam; (social), Dear Lady S—.
Spoken, Lady S—.

COUNTESS IN OWN RIGHT
As for an Earl's wife.

COURTESY TITLES

The heir apparent to a Duke, Marquess or Earl uses the highest of
his father's other titles as a courtesy title. The holder of a courtesy
title is not styled The Most Hon. or The Right Hon., and in
correspondence 'The' is omitted before the title. The heir
apparent to a Scottish title may use the title 'Master' (*see* below).

DAME

Envelope, Dame F— S—, followed by appropriate post-nominal
letters.
Letter (formal), Dear Madam; (social), Dear Dame F—.
Spoken, Dame F—.

DUKE

Envelope (formal), His Grace the Duke of—; (social), The Duke
of—.
Letter (formal), My Lord Duke; (social), Dear Duke.
Spoken (formal), Your Grace; (social), Duke.

DUKE'S WIFE

Envelope (formal), Her Grace the Duchess of—; (social), The
Duchess of—.
Letter (formal), Dear Madam; (social), Dear Duchess.
Spoken, Duchess.

DUKE'S ELDEST SON

See Courtesy titles.

DUKE'S YOUNGER SONS

Envelope, Lord F— S—.
Letter (formal), My Lord; (social), Dear Lord F—.
Spoken (formal), My Lord; (social), Lord F—.

DUKE'S DAUGHTER

Envelope, Lady F— S—.
Letter (formal), Dear Madam; (social), Dear Lady F—.
Spoken, Lady F—.

EARL

Envelope (formal), The Right Hon. the Earl (of)—; (social), The
Earl (of)—.
Letter (formal), My Lord; (social), Dear Lord—.
Spoken (formal), My Lord; (social), Lord—.

EARL'S WIFE

Envelope (formal), The Right Hon. the Countess (of)—; (social),
The Countess (of) —.
Letter (formal), Madam; (social), Lady—.
Spoken (formal), Madam; (social), Lady—.

EARL'S CHILDREN
Eldest son, *see* Courtesy titles.
Younger sons, The Hon. F— S— (for forms of address, *see* Baron's children).
Daughters, Lady F— S— (for forms of address, *see* Duke's daughter).

KNIGHT (BACHELOR)
Envelope, Sir F— S—.
Letter (formal), Dear Sir; (social), Dear Sir F—.
Spoken, Sir F—.

KNIGHT (ORDERS OF CHIVALRY)
Envelope, Sir F— S—, followed by appropriate post-nominal letters.
Otherwise as for Knight Bachelor.

KNIGHT'S WIFE
As for Baronet's wife.

LIFE PEER
As for Baron or for Baroness in own right.

LIFE PEER'S WIFE
As for Baron's wife.

LIFE PEER'S CHILDREN
As for Baron's children.

MARQUESS
Envelope (formal), The Most Hon. the Marquess of—; (social), The Marquess of—.
Letter (formal), My Lord; (social), Dear Lord—.
Spoken (formal), My Lord; (social), Lord—.

MARQUESS'S WIFE
Envelope (formal), The Most Hon. the Marchioness of—; (social), The Marchioness of—.
Letter (formal), Madam; (social), Dear Lady—.
Spoken, Lady—.

MARQUESS'S CHILDREN
Eldest son, *see* Courtesy titles.
Younger sons, Lord F— S— (for forms of address, *see* Duke's younger sons).
Daughters, Lady F— S— (for forms of address, *see* Duke's daughter).

Master

The title is used by the heir apparent to a Scottish peerage, though usually the heir apparent to a Duke, Marquess or Earl uses his courtesy title rather than 'Master'.

Envelope, The Master of—.

Letter (formal), Dear Sir; (social), Dear Master of—.

Spoken (formal), Master, or Sir; (social), Master, or Mr S—.

Master's Wife

Addressed as for the wife of the appropriate peerage style, otherwise as Mrs S—.

Privy Counsellor

Envelope, The Right (or Rt.) Hon. F— S—.

Letter, Dear Mr/Miss/Mrs S—.

Spoken, Mr/Miss/Mrs S—.

It is incorrect to use the letters PC after the name in conjunction with the prefix The Right Hon., unless the Privy Counsellor is a peer below the rank of Marquess and so is styled The Right Hon. because of his rank. In this case only, the post-nominal letters may be used in conjunction with the prefix The Right Hon.

Viscount

Envelope (formal), The Right Hon. the Viscount—; (social), The Viscount—.

Letter (formal), My Lord; (social), Dear Lord—.

Spoken, Lord—.

Viscount's Wife

Envelope (formal), The Right Hon. the Viscountess—; (social), The Viscountess—.

Letter (formal), Madam; (social), Dear Lady—.

Spoken, Lady—.

Viscount's Children

As for Baron's children.

ORDER OF POSTNOMINAL INITIALS

Postnominal initials appear in the following order:

1 Orders and decorations conferred by the Crown (*see* below)
2 Appointments to The Queen, e.g. PC, ADC
3 University degrees
4 Religious orders, e.g. OSB, SJ
5 Medical qualifications (see below)
6 Fellowships of learned societies
7 Royal academies of art
8 Fellowships of professional institutions, associations
9 Writers to the Signet (WS)
10 Appointments (see below)
11 Memberships of the armed forces

ORDERS AND DECORATIONS

Bt. (Baronet) precedes all other letters after the surname
Kt. (Knight Bachelor) (postnominal initials not usually used)

VC	Victoria Cross
GC	George Cross

ORDERS OF CHIVALRY, ETC.

Initials in parenthesis are of honours no longer awarded, though holders of these honours may still be alive

KG	Knight/Lady Companion of the Order of the Garter
KT	Knight of the Order of the Thistle
(KP)	Knight of the Order of St Patrick
GCB	Knight/Dame Grand Cross of the Order of the Bath
OM	Order of Merit
(GCSI)	Knight Grand Commander of the Order of the Star of India
GCMG	Knight/Dame Grand Cross of the Order of St Michael and St George
(GCIE)	Knight Grand Commander of the Order of the Indian Empire
(CI)	Order of the Crown of India
GCVO	Knight/Dame Grand Cross of the Royal Victorian Order
GBE	Knight/Dame Grand Cross of the Order of the British Empire
CH	Companion of Honour
KCB/DCB	Knight/Dame Commander of the Order of the Bath
(KCSI)	Knight Commander of the Order of the Star of India

KCMG/DCMG	Knight/Dame Commander of the Order of St Michael and St George
(KCIE)	Knight Commander of the Order of the Indian Empire
KCVO/DCVO	Knight/Dame Commander of the Royal Victorian Order
KBE/DBE	Knight/Dame Commander of the Order of the British Empire
CB	Companion of the Order of the Bath
(CSI)	Companion of the Order of the Star of India
CMG	Companion of the Order of St Michael and St George
(CIE)	Companion of the Order of the Indian Empire
CVO	Commander of the Royal Victorian Order
CBE	Commander of the Order of the British Empire
DSO	Distinguished Service Order
LVO	Lieutenant of the Royal Victorian Order
OBE	Officer of the Order of the British Empire
(ISO)	Imperial Service Order
MVO	Member of the Royal Victorian Order
MBE	Member of the Order of the British Empire

DECORATIONS

CGC	Conspicuous Gallantry Cross
DSC	Distinguished Service Cross
MC	Military Cross
DFC	Distinguished Flying Cross
AFC	Air Force Cross

OTHER MEDALS*

DCM	Distinguished Conduct Medal
CGM	Conspicuous Gallantry Medal
GM	George Medal
QPM	Queen's Police Medal for gallantry
DSM	Distinguished Service Medal
MM	Military Medal
DFM	Distinguished Flying Medal
AFM	Air Force Medal
CPM	Colonial Police Medal for gallantry
RVM	Royal Victorian Medal
BEM	British Empire Medal
QPM	Queen's Police Medal for distinguished service
QFSM	Queen's Fire Service Medal for distinguished service

EFFICIENCY AND LONG SERVICE DECORATIONS, ETC.*

ERD	Army Emergency Reserve Decoration
(VD)	Volunteer Officers' Decoration
TD	Territorial Decoration
ED	Efficiency Decoration
RD	Decoration for Officers of the Royal Naval Reserve
(VRD)	Decoration for Officers of the Royal Naval Volunteer Reserve
AE	Air Efficiency Award

MEDICAL QUALIFICATIONS*

DM	Doctor of Medicine
MD	Doctor of Medicine
D.Ch.	Doctor of Surgery
FRCP	Fellow of the Royal College of Physicians
FRCPEd.	Fellow of the Royal College of Physicians of Edinburgh
FRCPI	Fellow of the Royal College of Physicians of Ireland
FRCP(Glas.)	Fellow of the Royal College of Physicians of Glasgow
FRCS	Fellow of the Royal College of Surgeons
FRCSEd.	Fellow of the Royal College of Surgeons of Edinburgh
FRCSI	Fellow of the Royal College of Surgeons of Ireland
FRCS(Glas.)	Fellow of the Royal College of Surgeons of Glasgow
FRCOG	Fellow of the Royal College of Obstetricians and Gynaecologists
FRCGP	Fellow of the Royal College of General Practitioners
FRCPath.	Fellow of the Royal College of Pathologists
FRCPsych.	Fellow of the Royal College of Psychiatrists
FRCR	Fellow of the Royal College of Radiologists
FRCA	Fellow of the Royal College of Anaesthetists
FDS	Fellow in Dental Surgery
FFCM	Fellow of the Faculty of Community Medicine

APPOINTMENTS

In the following order:

QC	Queen's Counsel (until appointed to the High Court)

MP	Member of Parliament
JP	Justice of the Peace
DL	Deputy Lord Lieutenant

*These lists are not all-inclusive but contain the most commonly awarded medals, decorations and qualifications.

RANKS IN THE ARMED FORCES

(The numbers indicate equivalent ranks in each service)

ROYAL NAVY
1 Admiral of the Fleet
2 Admiral (Adm.)
3 Vice-Admiral (Vice-Adm.)
4 Rear-Admiral (Rear-Adm.)
5 Commodore (Cdre)
6 Captain (Capt.)
7 Commander (Cdr.)
8 Lieutenant-Commander (Lt.-Cdr.)
9 Lieutenant (Lt.)
10 Sub-Lieutenant (Sub-Lt.)
11 Acting Sub-Lieutenant (Acting Sub-Lt.)

ARMY
1 Field Marshal
2 General (Gen.)
3 Lieutenant-General (Lt.-Gen.)
4 Major-General (Maj.-Gen.)
5 Brigadier (Brig.)
6 Colonel (Col.)
7 Lieutenant-Colonel (Lt.-Col.)
8 Major (Maj.)
9 Captain (Capt.)
10 Lieutenant (Lt.)
11 Second Lieutenant (2nd Lt.)

ROYAL AIR FORCE
1 Marshal of the RAF
2 Air Chief Marshal
3 Air Marshal
4 Air Vice-Marshal
5 Air Commodore (Air Cdre)
6 Group Captain (Gp Capt)
7 Wing Commander (Wg Cdr.)
8 Squadron Leader (Sqn. Ldr.)
9 Flight Lieutenant (Flt. Lt.)
10 Flying Officer (FO)
11 Pilot Officer (PO)

FLAG-FLYING DAYS
ON GOVERNMENT BUILDINGS

The correct orientation of the Union Flag when flying is with the broader diagonal band of white uppermost in the hoist (i.e. near the pole) and the narrower diagonal band of white uppermost in the fly (i.e. furthest from the pole).

It is the practice to fly the Union Flag daily on some customs houses. In all other cases, flags are flown on government buildings by command of The Queen.

Days for hoisting the Union Flag are notified to the Department of Culture, Media and Sport by The Queen's command and communicated by the department to the other government departments. On the days appointed, the Union Flag is flown on government buildings in the United Kingdom from 8 a.m. to sunset.

6 February	The Queen's Accession
19 February	Birthday of The Duke of York
1 March	St David's Day (in Wales only)★
10 March	Birthday of The Earl of Wessex
13 March	Commonwealth Day (2000; second Monday in March each year)
21 April	Birthday of The Queen
23 April	St George's Day (in England only)★
9 May	Europe Day
2 June	Coronation Day
10 June	Birthday of The Duke of Edinburgh
10 June	The Queen's Official Birthday (2000; date varies)
4 August	Birthday of Queen Elizabeth the Queen Mother
15 August	Birthday of The Princess Royal
21 August	Birthday of The Princess Margaret
12 November	Remembrance Sunday (2000; date varies)
14 November	Birthday of The Prince of Wales
20 November	The Queen's Wedding Day
30 November	St Andrew's Day (in Scotland only)★

The opening of Parliament by The Queen†
The prorogation of Parliament by The Queen†

★Where a building has two or more flagstaffs, the appropriate national/European Union flag may be flown in addition to the Union Flag, but not in a superior position

†Flags are flown whether or not The Queen performs the ceremony in person. Flags are flown only in the Greater London area

FLAGS AT HALF-MAST

Flags are flown at half-mast on the following occasions:

(a)   From the announcement of the death up to the funeral of the Sovereign, except on Proclamation Day, when flags are hoisted right up from 11 a.m. to sunset

(b)   The funerals of members of the Royal Family, subject to special commands from The Queen in each case

(c)   The funerals of foreign rulers, subject to special commands from The Queen in each case

(d)   The funerals of Prime Ministers and ex-Prime Ministers of the United Kingdom, subject to special commands from The Queen in each case

(e)   Other occasions by special command of The Queen

On occasions when days for flying flags coincide with days for flying flags at half-mast, the following rules are observed. Flags are flown:

(a)   although a member of the Royal Family, or a near relative of the Royal Family, may be lying dead, unless special commands be received from The Queen to the contrary

(b)   although it may be the day of the funeral of a foreign ruler

If the body of a very distinguished subject is lying at a government office, the flag may fly at half-mast on that office until the body has left (provided it is a day on which the flag would fly) and then the flag is to be hoisted right up. On all other government buildings the flag will fly as usual.

THE ROYAL STANDARD

The Royal Standard is hoisted only when The Queen is actually present in the building, and never when Her Majesty is passing in procession.

SPORT

THE COMMONWEALTH GAMES

The Games were originally called the British Empire Games.
From 1954 to 1966 the Games were known as the British Empire
and Commonwealth Games, and from 1970 to 1974 as the
British Commonwealth Games. Since 1978 the Games have been
called the Commonwealth Games.

BRITISH EMPIRE GAMES

1930   Hamilton, Canada
1934   London, England
1938   Sydney, Australia
1950   Auckland, New Zealand

BRITISH EMPIRE AND COMMONWEALTH GAMES

1954   Vancouver, Canada
1958   Cardiff, Wales
1962   Perth, Australia
1966   Kingston, Jamaica

BRITISH COMMONWEALTH GAMES

1970   Edinburgh, Scotland
1974   Christchurch, New Zealand

COMMONWEALTH GAMES

1978   Edmonton, Canada
1982   Brisbane, Australia
1986   Edinburgh, Scotland
1990   Auckland, New Zealand
1994   Victoria, Canada
1998   Kuala Lumpur, Malaysia
2002   Manchester, England

THE OLYMPIC GAMES

MODERN OLYMPIC GAMES

1896   Athens, Greece
1900   Paris, France
1904   St Louis, USA
1908   London, Britain
1912   Stockholm, Sweden
1920   Antwerp, Belgium
1924   Paris, France
1928   Amsterdam, Netherlands

1932	Los Angeles, USA
1936	Berlin, Germany
1948	London, Britain
1952	Helsinki, Finland
1956	Melbourne, Australia
	(equestrian events held in Stockholm, Sweden)
1960	Rome, Italy
1964	Tokyo, Japan
1968	Mexico City, Mexico
1972	Munich, West Germany
1976	Montreal, Canada
1980	Moscow, USSR
1984	Los Angeles, USA
1988	Seoul, South Korea
1992	Barcelona, Spain
1996	Atlanta, USA
2000	Sydney, Australia
2004	Athens, Greece

The following Games were scheduled but did not take place owing to World Wars:

1916	Berlin, Germany
1940	Tokyo, Japan; then Helsinki, Finland
1944	London, Britain

WINTER OLYMPIC GAMES

1924	Chamonix, France
1928	St Moritz, Switzerland
1932	Lake Placid, USA
1936	Garmisch-Partenkirchen, Germany
1948	St Moritz, Switzerland
1952	Oslo, Norway
1956	Cortina d'Ampezzo, Italy
1960	Squaw Valley, USA
1964	Innsbruck, Austria
1968	Grenoble, France
1972	Sapporo, Japan
1976	Innsbruck, Austria
1980	Lake Placid, USA
1984	Sarajevo, Yugoslavia
1988	Calgary, Canada
1992	Albertville, France
1994	Lillehammer, Norway
1998	Nagano, Japan
2002	Salt Lake City, USA
2006	Turin, Italy

ATHLETICS

WORLD RECORDS AS AT 30 JUNE 1999

All the world records given below have been accepted by the International Amateur Athletic Federation except those marked with an asterisk★ which are awaiting homologation. Fully automatic timing to 1/100th second is mandatory up to and including 400 m. For distances up to and including 10,000 m, records will be accepted to 1/100th second if timed automatically, and to 1/10th if hand timing is used.

MEN

Track Events

100 m	9.79 sec	1999	Maurice Green (USA)
200 m	19.32 sec	1996	Michael Johnson (USA)
400 m	43.29 sec	1988	Butch Reynolds (USA)
800 m	1 min 41.11 sec	1997	Wilson Kipketer (Denmark)
1,000 m	2 min 12.18 sec	1981	Sebastian Coe (GB)
1,500 m	3 min 26.00 sec	1998	Hicham El Guerouj (Morocco)
1 mile	3 min 44.39 sec	1993	Noureddine Morceli (Algeria)
2,000 m	4 min 47.88 sec	1995	Noureddine Morceli (Algeria)
3,000 m	7 min 20.67 sec	1996	Daniel Komen (Kenya)
5,000 m	12 min 39.36 sec	1998	Haile Gebrselassie (Ethiopia)
10,000 m	26 min 22.75 sec	1998	Haile Gebrselassie (Ethiopia)
25,000 m	1 h 13 m 55.8 s	1981	Toshihiko Seko (Japan)
30,000 m	1 h 29 m 18.8 s	1981	Toshihiko Seko (Japan)
110 m hurdles	12.91 sec	1993	Colin Jackson (GB)
400 m hurdles	46.78 sec	1992	Kevin Young (USA)
3,000 m steeplechase	7 min 55.72 sec	1997	Bernard Barmasai (Kenya)

Relays

4 x 100 m	37.40 sec	1992, 1993	USA
4 x 400 m	2 min 54.20 sec	1998	USA

Field Events

High jump	2.45 m	1993	Javier Sotomayor (Cuba)
Pole vault	6.14 m	1994	Sergei Bubka (Ukraine)
Long jump	8.95 m	1991	Mike Powell (USA)
Triple jump	18.29 m	1995	Jonathan Edwards (GB)
Shot	23.12 m	1990	Randy Barnes (USA)
Discus	74.08 m	1986	Jürgen Schult (GDR)
Hammer	86.74 m	1986	Yuriy Sedykh (USSR)
Javelin	98.48 m	1996	Jan Zelezny (Czech Republic)
Decathlon	8,891 points	1992	Dan O'Brien (USA)

WOMEN

Track Events

100 m	10.49 sec	1988	Florence Griffith-Joyner (USA)
200 m	21.34 sec	1988	Florence Griffith-Joyner (USA)
400 m	47.60 sec	1985	Marita Koch (GDR)
800 m	1 min 53.28 sec	1983	Jarmila Kratochvilova (Czechoslovakia)
1,500 m	3 min 50.46 sec	1993	Qu Yunxia (China)
1 mile	4 min 12.56 sec	1996	Svetlana Masterkova (Russia)
3,000 m	8 min 06.11 sec	1993	Wang Junxia (China)
5,000 m	14 min 28.09 sec	1997	Jiang Bo (China)
10,000 m	29 min 31.78 sec	1993	Wang Junxia (China)
100 m hurdles	12.21 sec	1988	Yordanka Donkova (Bulgaria)
400 m hurdles	52.61 sec	1995	Kim Batten (USA)

Relays

4 x 100 m	41.37 sec	1985	GDR
4 x 400 m	3 min 15.17 sec	1988	USSR

Field Events

High jump	2.09 m	1987	Stefka Kostadinova (Bulgaria)
Pole vault	4.60 m	1999	Emma George (Australia)
Long jump	7.52 m	1988	Galina Chistiakova (USSR)

Triple jump	15.50 m	1995	Inessa Kravets (Ukraine)
Shot	22.63 m	1987	Natalya Lisovskaya (USSR)
Discus	76.80 m	1988	Gabriele Reinsch (GDR)
Hammer	75.97 m	1999	Mihaela Melinte (Romania)
Javelin	80.00 m	1988	Petra Felke (GDR)
Heptathlon	7,291 points	1988	Jackie Joyner-Kersee (USA)

UK RECORDS AS AT 30 JUNE 1999

Records set anywhere by athletes eligible to represent Great Britain and Northern Ireland

MEN

Track Events

100 m	9.87 sec	1993	Linford Christie
200 m	19.87 sec	1994	John Regis
400 m	44.36 sec	1997	Iwan Thomas
800 m	1 min 41.73 sec	1981	Sebastian Coe
1,000 m	2 min 12.18 sec	1981	Sebastian Coe
1,500 m	3 min 29.67 sec	1985	Sebastian Coe
1 mile	3 min 46.32 sec	1985	Steve Cram
2,000 m	4 min 51.39 sec	1985	Steve Cram
3,000 m	7 min 32.79 sec	1982	David Moorcroft
5,000 m	13 min 00.41 sec	1982	David Moorcroft
10,000 m	27 min 18.14 sec	1998	Jon Brown
25,000 m	1 h 15 m 22.6 s	1965	Ron Hill
30,000 m	1 h 31 m 30.4 s	1970	Jim Alder
110 m hurdles	12.91 sec	1993	Colin Jackson
400 m hurdles	47.82 sec	1992	Kriss Akabusi
3,000 m steeplechase	8 min 07.96 sec	1988	Mark Rowland

Relays

| 4 x 100 m | 37.77 sec | 1993 | GB team |
| 4 x 400 m | 2 min 56.60 sec | 1996 | GB team |

Field Events

High jump	2.37 m	1992, 1993	Steve Smith
Pole vault	5.80 m*	1998	Nick Buckfield
Long jump	8.23 m	1968	Lynn Davies
Triple jump	18.29 m	1995	Jonathan Edwards

Shot	21.68 m	1980	Geoff Capes
Discus	66.64 m★	1998	Perris Wilkins
Hammer	77.54 m	1984	Martin Girvan
Javelin	91.46 m	1992	Steve Backley
Decathlon	8,847 points	1984	Daley Thompson

WOMEN

Track Events

100 m	11.10 sec	1981	Kathy Cook
200 m	22.10 sec	1984	Kathy Cook
400 m	49.43 sec	1984	Kathy Cook
800 m	1 min 56.21 sec	1995	Kelly Holmes
1,500 m	3 min 58.07 sec	1997	Kelly Holmes
1 mile	4 min 17.57 sec	1985	Zola Budd
3,000 m	8 min 28.83 sec	1985	Zola Budd
5,000 m	14 min 45.51 sec	1997	Paula Radcliffe
10,000 m	30 min 40.70 sec★	1999	Paula Radcliffe
100 m hurdles	12.80 sec	1996	Angela Thorp
400 m hurdles	52.74 sec	1993	Sally Gunnell

Relays

4 x 100 m	42.43 sec	1980	GB team
4 x 400 m	3 min 22.01 sec	1991	GB team

Field Events

High jump	1.95 m	1982	Diana Elliott
Pole vault	4.31 m	1998	Janine Whitlock
Long jump	6.90 m	1983	Beverley Kinch
Triple jump	15.15 m	1997	Ashia Hansen
Shot	19.36 m	1988	Judy Oakes
Discus	67.48 m	1981	Margaret Ritchie
Hammer	66.75 m	1999	Lorraine Shaw
Javelin	77.44 m	1986	Fatima Whitbread
Heptathlon	6,736 points	1997	Denise Lewis

★Awaiting ratification

CRICKET

WORLD CUP WINNERS

First held 1975

Year	Winner
1975	West Indies
1979	West Indies
1983	India
1987	Australia

1992	Pakistan
1996	Sri Lanka
1999	Australia

COUNTY CHAMPIONS SINCE 1950

First held 1864

Year	Winner
1950	Lancashire/Surrey
1951	Warwickshire
1952	Surrey
1953	Surrey
1954	Surrey
1955	Surrey
1956	Surrey
1957	Surrey
1958	Surrey
1959	Yorkshire
1960	Yorkshire
1961	Hampshire
1962	Yorkshire
1963	Yorkshire
1964	Worcestershire
1965	Worcestershire
1966	Yorkshire
1967	Yorkshire
1968	Yorkshire
1969	Glamorgan
1970	Kent
1971	Surrey
1972	Warwickshire
1973	Hampshire
1974	Worcestershire
1975	Leicestershire
1976	Middlesex
1977	Kent/Middlesex
1978	Kent
1979	Essex
1980	Middlesex
1981	Nottinghamshire
1982	Middlesex
1983	Essex
1984	Essex
1985	Middlesex
1986	Essex
1987	Nottinghamshire
1988	Worcestershire
1989	Worcestershire

Year	Winner
1990	Middlesex
1991	Essex
1992	Essex
1993	Middlesex
1994	Warwickshire
1995	Warwickshire
1996	Leicestershire
1997	Glamorgan
1998	Leicestershire

FOOTBALL

WORLD CUP WINNERS

First held 1930

Year	Venue	Winner
1930	Uruguay	Uruguay
1934	Italy	Italy
1938	France	Italy
1950	Brazil	Uruguay
1954	Switzerland	West Germany
1958	Sweden	Brazil
1962	Chile	Brazil
1966	England	England
1970	Mexico	Brazil
1974	West Germany	West Germany
1978	Argentina	Argentina
1982	Spain	Italy
1986	Mexico	Argentina
1990	Italy	West Germany
1994	USA	Brazil
1998	France	France

LEAGUE CHAMPIONS SINCE 1950

First held 1889

Year	Winner
1950	Portsmouth
1951	Tottenham Hotspur
1952	Manchester United
1953	Arsenal
1954	Wolverhampton Wanderers
1955	Chelsea
1956	Manchester United
1957	Manchester United
1958	Wolverhampton Wanderers
1959	Wolverhampton Wanderers

1960	Burnley
1961	Tottenham Hotspur
1962	Ipswich Town
1963	Everton
1964	Liverpool
1965	Manchester United
1966	Liverpool
1967	Manchester United
1968	Manchester City
1969	Leeds United
1970	Everton
1971	Arsenal
1972	Derby County
1973	Liverpool
1974	Leeds United
1975	Derby County
1976	Liverpool
1977	Liverpool
1978	Nottingham Forest
1979	Liverpool
1980	Liverpool
1981	Aston Villa
1982	Liverpool
1983	Liverpool
1984	Liverpool
1985	Everton
1986	Liverpool
1987	Everton
1988	Liverpool
1989	Arsenal
1990	Liverpool
1991	Arsenal
1992	Leeds United
	Premiership
1993	Manchester United
1994	Manchester United
1995	Blackburn Rovers
1996	Manchester United
1997	Manchester United
1998	Arsenal
1999	Manchester United

FA CUP WINNERS SINCE 1950

First held 1872

Year	Winner
1950	Arsenal
1951	Newcastle United

Year	Winner
1952	Newcastle United
1953	Blackpool
1954	West Bromwich Albion
1955	Newcastle United
1956	Manchester City
1957	Aston Villa
1958	Bolton Wanderers
1959	Nottingham Forest
1960	Wolverhampton Wanderers
1961	Tottenham Hotspur
1962	Tottenham Hotspur
1963	Manchester United
1964	West Ham United
1965	Liverpool
1966	Everton
1967	Tottenham Hotspur
1968	West Bromwich Albion
1969	Manchester City
1970	Chelsea
1971	Arsenal
1972	Leeds United
1973	Sunderland
1974	Liverpool
1975	West Ham United
1976	Southampton
1977	Manchester United
1978	Ipswich Town
1979	Arsenal
1980	West Ham United
1981	Tottenham Hotspur
1982	Tottenham Hotspur
1983	Manchester United
1984	Everton
1985	Manchester United
1986	Liverpool
1987	Coventry
1988	Wimbledon
1989	Liverpool
1990	Manchester United
1991	Tottenham Hotspur
1992	Liverpool
1993	Arsenal
1994	Manchester United
1995	Everton
1996	Manchester United
1997	Chelsea
1998	Arsenal
1999	Manchester United

GOLF

THE OPEN CHAMPIONS SINCE 1950

First held 1860. Played over 72 holes since 1892

Year	Winner
1950	Bobby Locke (South Africa)
1951	Max Faulkner (GB)
1952	Bobby Locke (South Africa)
1953	Ben Hogan (USA)
1954	Peter Thomson (Australia)
1955	Peter Thomson (Australia)
1956	Peter Thomson (Australia)
1957	Bobby Locke (South Africa)
1958	Peter Thomson (Australia)
1959	Gary Player (South Africa)
1960	Kel Nagle (Australia)
1961	Arnold Palmer (USA)
1962	Arnold Palmer (USA)
1963	Bob Charles (New Zealand)
1964	Tony Lema (USA)
1965	Peter Thomson (Australia)
1966	Jack Nicklaus (USA)
1967	Roberto de Vicenzo (Argentina)
1968	Gary Player (South Africa)
1969	Tony Jacklin (GB)
1970	Jack Nicklaus (USA)
1971	Lee Trevino (USA)
1972	Lee Trevino (USA)
1973	Tom Weiskopf (USA)
1974	Gary Player (South Africa)
1975	Tom Watson (USA)
1976	Johnny Miller (USA)
1977	Tom Watson (USA)
1978	Jack Nicklaus (USA)
1979	Severiano Ballesteros (Spain)
1980	Tom Watson (USA)
1981	Bill Rogers (USA)
1982	Tom Watson (USA)
1983	Tom Watson (USA)
1984	Severiano Ballesteros (Spain)
1985	Sandy Lyle (GB)
1986	Greg Norman (Australia)
1987	Nick Faldo (GB)
1988	Severiano Ballesteros (Spain)
1989	Mark Calcavecchia (USA)
1990	Nick Faldo (GB)
1991	Ian Baker-Finch (Australia)
1992	Nick Faldo (GB)
1993	Greg Norman (Australia)

1994	Nick Price (Zimbabwe)
1995	John Daly (USA)
1996	Tom Lehman (USA)
1997	Justin Leonard (USA)
1998	Mark O'Meara (USA)
1999	Paul Lawrie (GB)

RYDER CUP WINNERS SINCE 1951

First held 1927. Played over 2 days 1927–61; over 3 days 1963 to date

Year	Winner
1951	USA
1953	USA
1955	USA
1957	Great Britain
1959	USA
1961	USA
1963	USA
1965	USA
1967	USA
1969	Match drawn
1971	USA
1973	USA
1975	USA
1977	USA
1979	USA
1981	USA
1983	USA
1985	Great Britain and Europe
1987	Great Britain and Europe
1989	Match drawn
1991	USA
1993	USA
1995	Europe
1997	Europe

US OPEN CHAMPIONS SINCE 1950

First held 1895

Year	Winner
1950	Ben Hogan (USA)
1951	Ben Hogan (USA)
1952	Julius Boros (USA)
1953	Ben Hogan (USA)
1954	Ed Furgol (USA)
1955	Jack Fleck (USA)
1956	Cary Middlecoff (USA)
1957	Dick Mayer (USA)
1958	Tommy Bolt (USA)

1959	Billy Casper (USA)
1960	Arnold Palmer (USA)
1961	Gene Littler (USA)
1962	Jack Nicklaus (USA)
1963	Julius Boros (USA)
1964	Ken Venturi (USA)
1965	Gary Player (South Africa)
1966	Billy Casper (USA)
1967	Jack Nicklaus (USA)
1968	Lee Trevino (USA)
1969	Orville Moody (USA)
1970	Tony Jacklin (GB)
1971	Lee Trevino (USA)
1972	Jack Nicklaus (USA)
1973	Johnny Miller (USA)
1974	Hale Irwin (USA)
1975	Lou Graham (USA)
1976	Jerry Pate (USA)
1977	Hubert Green (USA)
1978	Andy North (USA)
1979	Hale Irwin (USA)
1980	Jack Nicklaus (USA)
1981	David Graham (Australia)
1982	Tom Watson (USA)
1983	Larry Nelson (USA)
1984	Fuzzy Zoeller (USA)
1985	Andy North (USA)
1986	Raymond Floyd (USA)
1987	Scott Simpson (USA)
1988	Curtis Strange (USA)
1989	Curtis Strange (USA)
1990	Hale Irwin (USA)
1991	Payne Stewart (USA)
1992	Tom Kite (USA)
1993	Lee Janzen (USA)
1994	Ernie Els (South Africa)
1995	Corey Pavin (USA)
1996	Steve Jones (USA)
1997	Ernie Els (South Africa)
1998	Lee Janzen (USA)
1999	Payne Stewart (USA)

US MASTERS CHAMPIONS SINCE 1950

First held 1934

Year	Winner
1950	Jimmy Demaret (USA)
1951	Ben Hogan (USA)
1952	Sam Snead (USA)

Year	Winner
1953	Ben Hogan (USA)
1954	Sam Snead (USA)
1955	Cary Middlecoff (USA)
1956	Jack Burke Jnr (USA)
1957	Doug Ford (USA)
1958	Arnold Palmer (USA)
1959	Art Wall Jnr (USA)
1960	Arnold Palmer (USA)
1961	Gary Player (South Africa)
1962	Arnold Palmer (USA)
1963	Jack Nicklaus (USA)
1964	Arnold Palmer (USA)
1965	Jack Nicklaus (USA)
1966	Jack Nicklaus (USA)
1967	Gay Brewer (USA)
1968	Bob Goalby (USA)
1969	George Archer (USA)
1970	Billy Casper (USA)
1971	Charles Coody (USA)
1972	Jack Nicklaus (USA)
1973	Tommy Aaron (USA)
1974	Gary Player (South Africa)
1975	Jack Nicklaus (USA)
1976	Raymond Floyd (USA)
1977	Tom Watson (USA)
1978	Gary Player (South Africa)
1979	Fuzzy Zoeller (USA)
1980	Severiano Ballesteros (Spain)
1981	Tom Watson (USA)
1982	Craig Stadler (USA)
1983	Severiano Ballesteros (Spain)
1984	Ben Crenshaw (USA)
1985	Bernhard Langer (W. Germany)
1986	Jack Nicklaus (USA)
1987	Larry Mize (USA)
1988	Sandy Lyle (GB)
1989	Nick Faldo (GB)
1990	Nick Faldo (GB)
1991	Ian Woosnam (GB)
1992	Fred Couples (USA)
1993	Bernhard Langer (Germany)
1994	José María Olazábal (Spain)
1995	Ben Crenshaw (USA)
1996	Nick Faldo (GB)
1997	Tiger Woods (USA)
1998	Mark O'Meara (USA)
1999	José María Olazábal (Spain)

HORSE RACING

DERBY WINNERS SINCE 1950

The Derby was first run in 1780

Year	Winning horse
1950	Galcador
1951	Arctic Prince
1952	Tulyar
1953	Pinza
1954	Never Say Die
1955	Phil Drake
1956	Lavandin
1957	Crepello
1958	Hard Ridden
1959	Parthia
1960	St Paddy
1961	Psidium
1962	Larkspur
1963	Relko
1964	Santa Claus
1965	Sea Bird II
1966	Charlottown
1967	Royal Palace
1968	Sir Ivor
1969	Blakeney
1970	Nijinsky
1971	Mill Reef
1972	Roberto
1973	Morston
1974	Snow Knight
1975	Grundy
1976	Empery
1977	The Minstrel
1978	Shirley Heights
1979	Troy
1980	Henbit
1981	Shergar
1982	Golden Fleece
1983	Teenoso
1984	Secreto
1985	Slip Anchor
1986	Shahrastani
1987	Reference Point
1988	Kahyasi
1989	Nashwan
1990	Quest for Fame
1991	Generous
1992	Dr Devious
1993	Commander In Chief

Year	Winning horse
1994	Erhaab
1995	Lammtarra
1996	Shaamit
1997	Benny The Dip
1998	High Rise
1999	Oath

GRAND NATIONAL WINNERS SINCE 1950

The Grand National was first run in 1839

Year	Winning horse
1950	Freebooter
1951	Nickel Coin
1952	Teal
1953	Early Mist
1954	Royal Tan
1955	Quare Times
1956	ESB
1957	Sundew
1958	Mr What
1959	Oxo
1960	Merryman II
1961	Nicolaus Silver
1962	Kilmore
1963	Ayala
1964	Team Spirit
1965	Jay Trump
1966	Anglo
1967	Foinavon
1968	Red Alligator
1969	Highland Wedding
1970	Gay Trip
1971	Specify
1972	Well To Do
1973	Red Rum
1974	Red Rum
1975	L'Escargot
1976	Rag Trade
1977	Red Rum
1978	Lucius
1979	Rubstic
1980	Ben Nevis
1981	Aldaniti
1982	Grittar
1983	Corbiere
1984	Hallo Dandy
1985	Last Suspect
1986	West Tip

1987	Maori Venture
1988	Rhyme 'N' Reason
1989	Little Polveir
1990	Mr Frisk
1991	Seagram
1992	Party Politics
1993	Race declared void
1994	Miinnehoma
1995	Royal Athlete
1996	Rough Quest
1997	Lord Gyllene
1998	Earth Summit
1999	Bobbyjo

MOTOR RACING

FORMULA ONE WORLD CHAMPIONS

First held 1950

Year	Winner
1950	Giuseppe Farina (Italy)
1951	Juan Manuel Fangio (Argentina)
1952	Alberto Ascari (Italy)
1953	Alberto Ascari (Italy)
1954	Juan Manuel Fangio (Argentina)
1955	Juan Manuel Fangio (Argentina)
1956	Juan Manuel Fangio (Argentina)
1957	Juan Manuel Fangio (Argentina)
1958	Mike Hawthorn (GB)
1959	Jack Brabham (Australia)
1960	Jack Brabham (Australia)
1961	Phil Hill (USA)
1962	Graham Hill (GB)
1963	Jim Clark (GB)
1964	John Surtees (GB)
1965	Jim Clark (GB)
1966	Jack Brabham (Australia)
1967	Denny Hulme (New Zealand)
1968	Graham Hill (GB)
1969	Jackie Stewart (GB)
1970	Jochen Rindt (Austria)
1971	Jackie Stewart (GB)
1972	Emerson Fittipaldi (Brazil)
1973	Jackie Stewart (GB)
1974	Emerson Fittipaldi (Brazil)
1975	Niki Lauda (Austria)
1976	James Hunt (GB)
1977	Niki Lauda (Austria)

Year	Winner
1978	Mario Andretti (USA)
1979	Jody Scheckter (South Africa)
1980	Alan Jones (Australia)
1981	Nelson Piquet (Brazil)
1982	Keke Rosberg (Finland)
1983	Nelson Piquet (Brazil)
1984	Niki Lauda (Austria)
1985	Alain Prost (France)
1986	Alain Prost (France)
1987	Nelson Piquet (Brazil)
1988	Ayrton Senna (Brazil)
1989	Alain Prost (France)
1990	Ayrton Senna (Brazil)
1991	Ayrton Senna (Brazil)
1992	Nigel Mansell (GB)
1993	Alain Prost (France)
1994	Michael Schumacher (Germany)
1995	Michael Schumacher (Germany)
1996	Damon Hill (GB)
1997	Jacques Villeneuve (Canada)
1998	Mika Hakkinen (Finland)

ROWING

THE UNIVERSITY BOAT RACE

First held 1829

1829–1998: Cambridge 75 wins, Oxford 68; 1 dead heat (1877)

Year	Winner
1980	Oxford
1981	Oxford
1982	Oxford
1983	Oxford
1984	Oxford
1985	Oxford
1986	Cambridge
1987	Oxford
1988	Oxford
1989	Oxford
1990	Oxford
1991	Oxford
1992	Oxford
1993	Cambridge
1994	Cambridge
1995	Cambridge
1996	Cambridge

1997   Cambridge
1998   Cambridge
1999   Cambridge

RUGBY LEAGUE

WORLD CUP WINNERS

First held 1954

Year	Winner
1954	Great Britain
1957	Australia
1960	Great Britain
1968	Australia
1970	Australia
1972	Great Britain
1975	Australia
1977	Australia
1988	Australia
1992	Australia
1995	Australia

CHALLENGE CUP WINNERS SINCE 1950

First held 1897

Year	Winner
1950	Warrington
1951	Wigan
1952	Workington Town
1953	Huddersfield
1954	Warrington
1955	Barrow
1956	St Helens
1957	Leeds
1958	Wigan
1959	Wigan
1960	Wakefield Trinity
1961	St Helens
1962	Wakefield Trinity
1963	Wakefield Trinity
1964	Widnes
1965	Wigan
1966	St Helens
1967	Featherstone Rovers
1968	Leeds
1969	Castleford
1970	Castleford

Year	Winner
1971	Leigh
1972	St Helens
1973	Featherstone Rovers
1974	Warrington
1975	Widnes
1976	St Helens
1977	Leeds
1978	Leeds
1979	Widnes
1980	Hull Kingston Rovers
1981	Widnes
1982	Hull
1983	Featherstone Rovers
1984	Widnes
1985	Wigan
1986	Castleford
1987	Halifax
1988	Wigan
1989	Wigan
1990	Wigan
1991	Wigan
1992	Wigan
1993	Wigan
1994	Wigan
1995	Wigan
1996	St Helens
1997	St Helens
1998	Sheffield
1999	Leeds

RUGBY UNION

WORLD CUP WINNERS

First held 1987

Year	Winner
1987	New Zealand
1991	Australia
1995	South Africa

FOUR/FIVE NATIONS CHAMPIONS SINCE 1950

First held 1883

Year	Winner
1950	Wales
1951	Ireland

1952	Wales
1953	England
1954	England/Wales/France
1955	Wales/France
1956	Wales
1957	England
1958	England
1959	France
1960	France/England
1961	France
1962	France
1963	England
1964	Scotland/Wales
1965	Wales
1966	Wales
1967	France
1968	France
1969	Wales
1970	Wales/France
1971	Wales
1972	Not completed
1973	Wales/Scotland/Ireland/England/France (5-way tie)
1974	Ireland
1975	Wales
1976	Wales
1977	France
1978	Wales
1979	Wales
1980	England
1981	France
1982	Ireland
1983	France/Ireland
1984	Scotland
1985	Ireland
1986	France/Scotland
1987	France
1988	Wales/France
1989	France
1990	Scotland
1991	England
1992	England
1993	France
1994	Wales
1995	England
1996	England
1997	France
1998	France
1999	Scotland

RFU KNOCK-OUT CUP WINNERS

First held 1972

Year	Winner
John Player Special Cup	
1972	Gloucester
1973	Coventry
1974	Coventry
1975	Bedford
1976	Gosforth
1977	Gosforth
1978	Gloucester
1979	Leicester
1980	Leicester
1981	Leicester
1982	Gloucester/Moseley
1983	Bristol
1984	Bath
1985	Bath
1986	Bath
1987	Bath
1988	Harlequins
Pilkington Cup	
1989	Bath
1990	Bath
1991	Harlequins
1992	Bath
1993	Leicester
1994	Bath
1995	Bath
1996	Bath
1997	Leicester
Tetley's Bitter Cup	
1998	Saracens
1999	Wasps

SNOOKER

WORLD PROFESSIONAL CHAMPIONS

First held 1927

Year	Winner
1950	Walter Donaldson (Scotland)
1951	Fred Davis (England)
1952	Horace Lindrum (Australia)

PROFESSIONAL MATCHPLAY CHAMPIONSHIP
1952	Fred Davis (England)

1953	Fred Davis (England)
1954	Fred Davis (England)
1955	Fred Davis (England)
1956	Fred Davis (England)
1957	John Pulman (England)

No championships were held 1958–63

CHALLENGE MATCHES

1964	John Pulman (England)
1965	John Pulman (England)
1966	John Pulman (England)
1967	John Pulman (England)
1968	John Pulman (England)

KNOCK-OUT

1969	John Spencer (England)
1970	Ray Reardon (Wales)
1971	John Spencer (England)
1972	Alex Higgins (N. Ireland)
1973	Ray Reardon (Wales)
1974	Ray Reardon (Wales)
1975	Ray Reardon (Wales)
1976	Ray Reardon (Wales)
1977	John Spencer (England)
1978	Ray Reardon (Wales)
1979	Terry Griffiths (Wales)
1980	Cliff Thorburn (Canada)
1981	Steve Davis (England)
1982	Alex Higgins (N. Ireland)
1983	Steve Davis (England)
1984	Steve Davis (England)
1985	Dennis Taylor (N. Ireland)
1986	Joe Johnson (England)
1987	Steve Davis (England)
1988	Steve Davis (England)
1989	Steve Davis (England)
1990	Stephen Hendry (Scotland)
1991	John Parrott (England)
1992	Stephen Hendry (Scotland)
1993	Stephen Hendry (Scotland)
1994	Stephen Hendry (Scotland)
1995	Stephen Hendry (Scotland)
1996	Stephen Hendry (Scotland)
1997	Ken Doherty (Ireland)
1998	John Higgins (Scotland)
1999	Stephen Hendry (Scotland)

TENNIS

WIMBLEDON MEN'S SINGLES CHAMPIONS
SINCE 1950

First held 1877

Year	Winner
1950	Budge Patty (USA)
1951	Dick Savitt (USA)
1952	Frank Sedgman (USA)
1953	Vic Seixas (USA)
1954	Jaroslav Drobny (Egypt)
1955	Tony Trabert (USA)
1956	Lew Hoad (Australia)
1957	Lew Hoad (Australia)
1958	Ashley Cooper (Australia)
1959	Alex Olmedo (USA)
1960	Neale Fraser (Australia)
1961	Rod Laver (Australia)
1962	Rod Laver (Australia)
1963	Chuck McKinley (USA)
1964	Roy Emerson (Australia)
1965	Roy Emerson (Australia)
1966	Manuel Santana (Spain)
1967	John Newcombe (Australia)
1968	Rod Laver (Australia)
1969	Rod Laver (Australia)
1970	John Newcombe (Australia)
1971	John Newcombe (Australia)
1972	Stan Smith (USA)
1973	Jan Kodes (Czechoslovakia)
1974	Jimmy Connors (USA)
1975	Arthur Ashe (USA)
1976	Bjorn Borg (Sweden)
1977	Bjorn Borg (Sweden)
1978	Bjorn Borg (Sweden)
1979	Bjorn Borg (Sweden)
1980	Bjorn Borg (Sweden)
1981	John McEnroe (USA)
1982	Jimmy Connors (USA)
1983	John McEnroe (USA)
1984	John McEnroe (USA)
1985	Boris Becker (W. Germany)
1986	Boris Becker (W. Germany)
1987	Pat Cash (Australia)
1988	Stefan Edberg (Sweden)
1989	Boris Becker (W. Germany)
1990	Stefan Edberg (Sweden)
1991	Michael Stich (Germany)
1992	Andre Agassi (USA)

1993	Pete Sampras (USA)
1994	Pete Sampras (USA)
1995	Pete Sampras (USA)
1996	Richard Krajicek (Netherlands)
1997	Pete Sampras (USA)
1998	Pete Sampras (USA)
1999	Pete Sampras (USA)

WIMBLEDON WOMEN'S SINGLES CHAMPIONS
SINCE 1950

First held 1884

Year	Winner
1950	Louise Brough (USA)
1951	Doris Hart (USA)
1952	Maureen Connolly (USA)
1953	Maureen Connolly (USA)
1954	Maureen Connolly (USA)
1955	Louise Brough (USA)
1956	Shirley Fry (USA)
1957	Althea Gibson (USA)
1958	Althea Gibson (USA)
1959	Maria Bueno (Brazil)
1960	Maria Bueno (Brazil)
1961	Angela Mortimer (GB)
1962	Karen Susman (USA)
1963	Margaret Smith (Australia)
1964	Maria Bueno (Brazil)
1965	Margaret Smith (Australia)
1966	Billie Jean King (USA)
1967	Billie Jean King (USA)
1968	Billie Jean King (USA)
1969	Ann Jones (GB)
1970	Margaret Court (Australia)
1971	Evonne Goolagong (Australia)
1972	Billie Jean King (USA)
1973	Billie Jean King (USA)
1974	Chris Evert (USA)
1975	Billie Jean King (USA)
1976	Chris Evert (USA)
1977	Virginia Wade (GB)
1978	Martina Navratilova (Czechoslovakia)
1979	Martina Navratilova (Czechoslovakia)
1980	Evonne Cawley (Australia)
1981	Chris Evert Lloyd (USA)
1982	Martina Navratilova (USA)
1983	Martina Navratilova (USA)
1984	Martina Navratilova (USA)
1985	Martina Navratilova (USA)
1986	Martina Navratilova (USA)

1987	Martina Navratilova (USA)
1988	Steffi Graf (W. Germany)
1989	Steffi Graf (W. Germany)
1990	Martina Navratilova (USA)
1991	Steffi Graf (Germany)
1992	Steffi Graf (Germany)
1993	Steffi Graf (Germany)
1994	Conchita Martinez (Spain)
1995	Steffi Graf (Germany)
1996	Steffi Graf (Germany)
1997	Martina Hingis (Switzerland)
1998	Jana Novotna (Czech Republic)
1999	Lindsay Davenport (USA)

YACHTING

AMERICA'S CUP WINNERS

First held 1870

Year	Winner
1870	Magic (USA)
1871	Columbia (USA)
	Sappho (USA)
1876	Madeleine (USA)
1881	Mischief (USA)
1885	Puritan (USA)
1886	Mayflower (USA)
1887	Volunteer (USA)
1893	Vigilant (USA)
1895	Defender (USA)
1899	Columbia (USA)
1901	Columbia (USA)
1903	Reliance (USA)
1920	Resolute (USA)
1930	Enterprise (USA)
1934	Rainbow (USA)
1937	Ranger (USA)
1958	Columbia (USA)
1962	Weatherly (USA)
1964	Constellation (USA)
1967	Intrepid (USA)
1970	Intrepid (USA)
1974	Courageous (USA)
1977	Courageous (USA)
1980	Freedom (USA)
1983	Australia II (Australia)
1987	Stars & Stripes (USA)
1988	Stars & Stripes (USA)
1992	America 3 (USA)
1995	Black Magic (New Zealand)